You Are More Than What You Weigh

IMPROVE YOUR SELF-ESTEEM
NO MATTER WHAT YOUR WEIGHT

Sharon Norfleet Sward, LPC

YOU ARE MORE
THAN WHAT YOU WEIGH

Improve Your Self-esteem No Matter What Your Weight

By Sharon Sward

Published by:
Wholesome Publisher
1231 S. Parker Rd. #102
Denver, CO 80231

Library of Congress Cataloging-in-Publication Data
Sward, Sharon
    You are more than what you weigh: improve your self-esteem no matter what your weight / Sharon Norfleet Sward. --2nd ed.
    p. cm.
    ISBN: 0-9648874-2-8

    1. Eating disorders--Psychological aspects. 2. Body image
    3. Obesity--Psychological aspects. 4. Self-esteem. I. Title

    BF697.5.B63S93 1998   616.85'26
                            QBI97-40894
    95-61855
                  CIP

I N T R O D U C T I O N

Why This Book is for You

$\mathcal{D}$o you want to learn to love yourself no matter what your weight? Is your identity based strictly on how much you weigh? Do you hate your whole body if you gain a pound? Do you tell yourself each morning that you are going to start a diet? Are you preoccupied with food, always thinking about what you are going to eat or not eat? If you were only thinner, do you believe that all of your problems would be resolved? If you answer "yes" to any of these questions, then You Are More Than What You Weigh is your answer.

Altering your weight may be unnecessary whether you are at your ideal weight, underweight, or overweight. Perhaps your true desire is to change how you feel about your body and self. This book discusses three major types of eating disorders: Anorexia nervosa, bulimia nervosa, and binge eating.(See appendix for characteristics of each.)

Since females tend to be more concerned about their weight than males, the word "she" refers to both sexes and in no way meant to discriminate against either sex. Males, however, will find this book helpful because it explains how their views of weight differ from females. In the era of managed-care-system, therapists will benefit because their clients can complete the exercises in this book between sessions.

■■■

How This Book Can Help You

You Are More Than What You Weigh is about improving your self-image. You don't have to be at your ideal weight in order to love yourself. If you have tried to lose weight and haven't succeeded in keeping it off, this book will help you understand the reasons behind your weight problems. It will give you the tools to help you make the changes you desire. If you are ambivalent about changing your eating habits and weight, you can benefit by changing your thoughts instead. Whether you are at your ideal weight, underweight, overweight, or purging, this book will aid you in becoming healthier. It can help you lose weight, stop starving, or end purging. More significantly, it will help you love yourself no matter what you weigh. This is about you...the most important person. You are valuable, lovable, and worthwhile. Even if you find it inconceivable now, you will believe it by the time you read and work through You Are More Than What You Weigh.

Unfortunately, society has conditioned us to think that thinner is better. One of the reasons you may have set yourself up for failure in the past is that you might have tied your identity to your weight. When you do this, you set yourself up for failure. Besides your weight or physical self, you want to value and identify yourself with the other aspects of yourself. These other aspects include the following ten types of selves:

   1. **Physical Self**   *(weight and body image)*
   2. **Intellectual Self**   *(your thoughts)*
   3. **Emotional Self**   *(your feelings)*
   4. **Social Self**   *(your relationships)*
   5. **Psychological Self**   *(identity and self-esteem)*
   6. **Spiritual Self**   *(higher power and values)*
   7. **Sexual Self**   *(male and female traits)*
   8. **Assertive Self**   *(not passive or aggressive)*
   9. **Stress/Relaxed Self**   *(stress causes and remedies)*
  10. **Career Self**   *(career analysis)*.

How these ten parts of yourself influence your weight, body image, eating, self-esteem, and exercises you can complete to resolve your issues are explained in this book. For example, compare yourself to a circle with ten equal parts. Your physical being is one piece of the circle along with the other nine parts. When all ten parts of yourself are equally

important, you and your live are balanced. You are not a well-rounded person when your physical self is the only important part of you.

Total Self

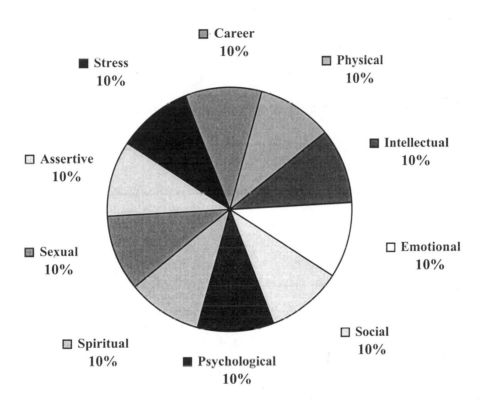

You are free to experience life in a new way when you are not consumed with your weight. You will learn to love and value all parts of yourself, improve your self-esteem, enhance your quality of life, and free yourself from the pressures of your weight.

Many find it is helpful to read the entire book prior to working on the exercises. You may choose to work on the exercises alone, with a friend, or in a group. I recommend you buy yourself a two or three-ring notebook and fill it with paper and dividers, one for each chapter in the book. If you prefer, you may purchase a workbook or a disk to use on your computer. Begin your journal by doing the exercises that are pertinent to you. You do not have to do them in any particular order. *Examples of what clients have said or what you may say to yourself at times have been italicized.* Simply add to the list how the topic applies to you. After the *italic statements,* therapist comments are underlined. For example:(From page 8)

11. Beliefs I can change about my body include:

   a. *I can tell myself I love my body.*
      (Fake it until you make it.)

   b. *I can love my body without it being perfect.*
      (Striving for a perfect body is an unrealistic goal.)

   c. *I can accept and love my body even if it isn't at my ideal weight.*
      (Loving your body is a step in reaching your ideal weight.)

At the end of each topic, you will find names of books related to the main ideas to provide you with additional help. As I have worked with my clients through the years, I noted their common characteristics, concerns and solutions. The solutions that worked for them are compiled in this book. Remember that life is a process. It has taken many years to develop your present patterns of behavior. Each day is a new day for you to change and to enjoy these changes. I wish you well in your journey to make your dreams come true and hope this book helps you become more than what you weigh.

Acknowledgement

*A*s a licensed professional counselor, I would like to thank my many clients whose experiences have helped me write this book. To my new friends on the Internet who have shared their experiences, I look forward to learning more from you. As president of Eating Disorder Professionals of Colorado, I have learned from our speakers, workshops, and professional friends. Thanks especially to Jeremy A. Lazarus, Larry Laycob, M.D., Susan Richardson, Ph.D. and Jack McInroe, Ed.D. for their supervision that helped me become the therapist I am today. My appreciation to my individual therapists, Dr. Robert Hoffman, Dr. Ralph E. Roughton and group leader Pat Penelton, who helped me in my personal development. Thanks also to Jill Mordini, Rosy Hughes, Kim Johansen, Pat Patterson, Amy Mauro and Ruth Astuno for their suggestions. I also want to thank my special friends now and in my past. I have had many great teachers, both in and out of the classroom that have taught me about life and myself. Last, but not least, thanks to my parents Myrtle and Leland Norfleet, my Aunt Madeline, my brothers Ken, Jerry, Jim, and John and my sister Karen. Thanks also to my husband Larry and two children, Brian and Melinda, for their patience during the writing of this book and continually teach me about being a parent and a wife.

What Professionals Say About This Book

National Eating Disorder Organization
Laureate Psychiatric Clinic Hospital Eating Disorders Program

You Are More Than What You Weigh is an inspirational and upbeat text expressing how women and men of today can learn to love themselves and improve self-image regardless of weight, size or shape. With great practical insight, Ms. Sward directs readers to begin to search internally for worth, instead of turning to food and others for satisfaction and comfort surrounding personal identity.

Each chapter is an excellent presentation of materials, exercises, and insights important for holistic and healthy treatment of weight management, rather than a magical formula promising weight loss and a happy life.

Ms. Sward's intensity throughout her book reflects her strong convictions for learning to love the self, regardless of body size or weight without being overly simplistic or matter-of-fact. Her personal experience, clinical vignettes and workbook-like exercises make this active, compassionate and practical book appropriate for use by clinicians as well as anyone else concerned about her weight and self-esteem.

The solution-focused approach Ms. Sward utilizes with obvious skill directly addresses the enigmatic question, "What can I do?" often asked by clients struggling with weight issues. The practical exercises in each chapter consist of thought-provoking questions and information, which provide invaluable direction and insights to the reader upon completion.

Certainly, this book is a valuable asset in the ever-present managed-care system, which continues to demand briefer and more solution-focused therapy. Because this text's purpose is less technical in nature, therapists may greatly benefit from referring clients to the exercises as homework between sessions.

In a time where healthy information about weight management is hard to come by, You Are More Than What You Weigh is an excellent tool for individual and group therapists, as well as appropriate reading for those clients looking for self-help and encouragement in overcoming the barriers to personal success.

Colorado Mental Health Counselors Association
Tamara Golden, President

You Are More Than What You Weigh is a book using a holistic perspective, emphasizing the fact that the physical self is only one aspect of a person and encourages readers to develop all dimensions of themselves. With continuing limits on third party payments for psychological services, therapy and between-session homework will assume greater importance as treatment modalities. This book is a valuable resource to assist clients in taking self-responsibility and giving them tools to use between counseling sessions.

Colorado Psychiatric Society
Deborah Stetler, M.D. Co-editor of the CPS and liaison to the
American Psychiatric Society Research Network

You Are More Than What You Weigh is a straightforward, no-nonsense series of written exercises to help persons with distorted eating discover other aspects of themselves (i.e., intellectual, social, spiritual). The book is based on the premise that once these other aspects are developed and valued, eating will take a more "normal" place in the person's life. Each exercise is preceded by a brief, easily understood discussion of the topic, followed by a series of questions. The exercises would be best used selectively and with guidance from the therapist. As we continue to emphasize the concept of "homework" between sessions, tools such as this book will become increasingly valued.

Columbia/Bethesda Eating Disorder Treatment Center-Denver
Kenneth Weiner, M.D. Medical Director at Bethesda Hospital in Denver
and Owner of Treatment Center

When looking at what causes Eating Disorders, poor self-esteem is frequently a critical contributor. You Are More Than What You Weigh is a practical and user friendly guide to help those with an eating disorder work on their sense of self and maximize their recovery. For anyone consumed by calories or weight, this handbook is a window to what you're really looking for.

Eating Disorder Professionals of Colorado
Richard Lindsey, Ph.D., CEAP; Past President of EDPC

You Are More Than What You Weigh is an affirmation and belief that permeates all aspects of this book and Ms. Sward's orientation toward recovery. Ms. Sward's approach is active, holistic and solution-focused. The book, in its presentation, is inherently hopeful, practical and helpful. Ms. Sward avoids simplistic and magical solutions to real and complex problems and does so in a loving, forgiving and accepting way.

National Ass. of Anorexia Nervosa & Associated Disorders
Vivian Meehan, President of ANAD

Happy to list your workbook in our bibliography since it is a worthwhile and helpful book. It is organized well and we believe it would be helpful to many.

The Children's Hospital
Jennifer Hagman, Medical Director

It is nice to have your book for our patients at Children's Hospital. There is a lot of valuable information in this book for them. I look forward to your future book specifically for adolescent and younger patients.

The Midwest Book Review
James A. Cox, Editor in Chief

You Are More Than What You Weigh is the ideal self-help guide for anyone concerned about their weight and self esteem. Whether the reader is female or male, adolescent or adult, anorexic, bulimic or a compulsive overeater, you will find You Are More Than What You Weigh a compendium of sound, practical advice, counsel and exercises. HIGHLY RECOMMENDED!

Clinical Nutrition Center
James Berry, M.D. Owner and President

You Are More Than What You Weigh is a wonderful resource for the many individuals who find themselves constantly preoccupied with what they weigh and what they eat. Poor self-esteem and image, loathing, and negative self-talk are pervasive in our weight obsessed society. While a significant 30 percent of American women are overweight, an astounding 70 percent believe they are fat. This 40 percent discrepancy between belief and reality is a terrible burden. Although traditionally considered primarily a problem of women, my twenty years experience treating the weight-obsessed convinces me it is an increasing problem for men.

This book will help you to understand your problem and how to deal with it effectively. While not specifically a weight loss manual, the lessons in this book will help you learn to control your weight more easily. Even greater value comes from improving your self-image and from not having your whole life controlled by what you weigh.

Weight*Choice*
Mike Bowers, Psy. D. Founder and Owner

You Are More Than What You Weigh is a wise and welcome gift of guidance for those of us who are determined to undo the damage of dieting in our own life and the lives of our loved ones.

Rocky Mountain News
Linda Castrone- Health and Fitness Editor

After ten years of leading eating disorder groups, Sharon Sward had developed more than a few exercises that helped drive home the point, You Are More Than What You Weigh. Her clients needed help learning to love themselves, no matter what the scales said.

People with eating disorders often focus on the physical self, excluding the other important parts of themselves. To help them start loving themselves physically, she suggests the following exercise: Think of things you can do to accept your body today, not waiting until you meet your ideal weight.

To overcome perfectionism, an intellectual trait common among people with eating disorders, she recommends: Think about how many ways you try to be perfect; perfect figure and clothes? Have to finish first or not at all? Feel pressure to achieve goals without making mistakes? Need to impress people in order to make them like you? Remember you don't have to excel at everything, that doing your best is more important than making a mistake.

Visualizations, journal writing, affirmations and having conversations with your problem are explained. Used as a whole, the book has something for just about everyone, with sections that range from the effect of abusive relationships on weight and learning from past successes and failures.

Comments from Readers

I was so thankful to have this book to help me through a difficult time. I feel it helped to save my life.

I felt understood. No judgment, just compassion and solutions for the problems my eating disorder has caused me.

I saw me in this book. What a relief to know I am not alone.

A book that gives me concrete solutions of what I can do for my issues.

I now have an understanding about what causes my eating disorder. Now I can do something about it.

Thanks for helping me to feel better about myself.

I plan to use this book for a long time. There is so much helpful information that I can use throughout my lifetime.

Thanks for sharing your experiences. It gives me encouragement that I, too can succeed.

I enjoyed your sharing what other people's experiences were.

I liked the suggested readings so I could look up additional readings.

Table of Contents

Tables and Forms

C H A P T E R   O N E

Accept and Love Your Body

So often individuals judge themselves according to their physical selves, which includes your looks, height, weight, body proportions, smile, posture, health, hair, nails, breasts, and how you carry yourself. By dwelling on the aspects of yourself that you cannot change and do not like, you begin to think negatively about yourself. You set yourself up to fail. This preoccupation with your physical self often sets you up for an eating disorder.

It is important to look at your health and eating habits when you think of your physical self. Although your physical being is only one part of you, it is important. You will feel better when you eat healthy and exercise, as well as look better. If you have dieted your entire life, you know that diets make you fat and work only as a temporary solution. Instead of dieting, develop eating habits you can follow the rest of your life.

You have probably asked yourself whether your food and weight problem was a result of inherited genes or your environment where your family taught eating behaviors. Both have a big influence. Your genes contribute to your looks, body's proportions, your metabolic rate, and your propensity to be overweight. It is important to accept your genes. You are also the product of behaviors your family taught you, such as eating patterns and style of eating. You can't change your genes, but you can change your behavior. Certainly, the older you are and the more diets you have been on in the past, the harder it is going to be to change your weight.

▰▰▰

It is becoming more accepted that some people have to live with being overweight. If you are one of these people, you may have to accept your body in a world that glamorizes thinness. Not everyone can be thin. To try to do so may cause more discomfort and stress than learning to love your body as it is. This does not mean that you don't eat healthily, but you accept that you may not be the weight you desire. It is important to see all aspects of you when thinking about yourself, not just your physical appearance. You are more than your physical being and more than what you weigh.

Improve Your Body Image

Body image is the perception you have of your body. People with eating disorders often have a distorted body image and perceive themselves to be larger than they are. When you lose weight but don't change your thoughts about your body, you have a distorted body image. You must start to accept and love your body now. If you don't like your body, you don't like who you are.

Anorexics have a distorted body image. Although they are underweight, they feel fat. Bulimics have a similar perspective. They perceive themselves as fat, although most are within ten pounds of their ideal weight. Most binge eaters think of themselves as much heavier than their real weight and a few view themselves smaller than what they are.

Compared to women, men are more realistic about their body image. Small men may desire to be larger, just as women desire to be smaller. This disturbance of men's body image is reverse anorexia. Some men perceive themselves as appearing small and weak, when in fact they are large and muscular. Some men with eating disorders begin weight lifting and steroid use to alter their small body images.

Love your body, no matter what you weigh. Each time that you go through a doorway, say, "Body, I love you," even if your belief is superficial and you hate your body. Continuing to say this, you will begin to believe it. One of my clients who did this (and she thought this was a ridiculous exercise at first) started getting comments about how much weight she had lost. She hadn't lost a pound, but she carried herself taller and with more confidence. It made her look lighter. It was only after she began loving her body, that she wanted to stop abusing it with junk food. She then began to lose weight she had never been able to lose before.

Start Today to Love Your Body

It is important to start loving yourself today, not waiting until you get to your desired weight. If you don't accept your body today, you will not feel differently about your body even as you lose weight. To accept and love your body today doesn't mean you have to keep it as is, but it does mean love it now. If you do not start to love your body, your body image will not change and you will become discouraged.

It is helpful to first concentrate on the part of the body you like the most. Once you learn to love that part, it is easier to generalize that feeling to other parts of your body. For example, if you like your eyes, look into the mirror and say, "I love you eyes. Thank you for seeing for me and being there for me." Then choose another part of your body. When you hate a part of your body, think about what its use is and how it would feel without it. For example, change the hate of your hips to the thought that hips are necessary for you to move. They also protect your organs inside your body. Thus, you are emphasizing what your body does that you like instead of how large they are. Continue to do this for each part of your body that you hate.

Value What Your Body
Does Instead of How It Looks

DISLIKES	LIKES	WHAT MY BODY DOES
Hips		*Allows legs to move and walk.*
	Arms	*Allows me to give hugs.*
Stomach		*Allows my food to be digested and provides a lap.*

3

DISLIKES	LIKES	WHAT MY BODY DOES
	Fingers	*Allows me to grasp things.*
Buttocks		*Allows me to sit.*
	Hair	*Protects my head from sunburn.*
Breast		*Allows me to breast-feed.*
	Legs	*Allows me to walk.*
Lips		*Allows me to kiss.*
	Ears	*Allows me to hear.*
Nose		*Helps me to smell.*
	Feet	*Helps me walk and keep my balance.*
Teeth		*Allows me to chew my food.*
	Waist	*Allows me to wear pretty belts.*

SELF EVALUATION:

1. **For every negative judgment that I say about my body, balance it with positive statements.**

   a. **My hips are too fat and round.**

   1. *My hips allow my legs to move.*
   2. *My round hips are better than those of my friend whose hips don't allow her to walk.*
   3. *My hips are large, but the rest of my body is not.*

   b. **My breasts are too large.**

   1. *My friend who had her breasts removed would probably be delighted to have any breasts, no matter what the size.*
   2. *My husband likes the fullness of my breasts.*
   3. *I can dress to take the accent away from my breasts.*

2. ***Make a list of people in my life who have had a major impact on the image I have of myself. How did they shape my attitude toward myself?**

   a. *Parents: Have always been on me about how underweight I am. (Anorexic)*
   b. *Brothers: Used to tease me about being fat. Although I was not fat, I thought of myself as fat because of their comments.*
   c. *Parents: Would not allow me to go places with them because they said that my weight embarrassed them.*

3. **What is some positive feedback I have received about my body? Do I allow these reactions to be received or do I discount them?**

   a. *I discount statements telling me I am thin. (Anorexic)*
   b. *I don't believe people when they tell me I do not need to lose weight. (Bulimic)*
   c. *It is difficult for me to hear compliments about my body.*
   d. *I discount comments which are made that I am pretty.*

4. **Imagine getting rid of the voice that says eat and I will feel better. What thinking can I use to replace it?**

   a. *There are other things besides eating to make me feel better such as calling a friend or writing in my journal.*
   b. *Food is a temporary fix; it is not a solution to the problem.*
   c. *Ask myself if I will feel better or worse after eating.*

5. **If my body could talk what would it say to me?**

   a. *My body feels like a car with all its parts worn out. It's hard to make it go anymore. (Anorexic)*
   b. *My body feels raw from throwing up all time. (Bulimic)*
   c. *My body is so tired from carrying all this weight. Please give me a break. (Binge eater)*

6. **What would I like to say to my body?**

   a. *Body, I am sorry I abuse you the way that I do. I would like to stop doing what I am doing to you, but right now I know no other way. However, I would like to make a contract with you that I make some changes and not abuse you so much. Please be patient with me.*
   b. *I am going to listen to my body to tell me when I am hungry and when I am full.*
   c. *I am tired of carrying all this extra weight. Let's try to work together body and mind instead of against each other.*

7. **Let my body become my friend instead of my object of fear or disgust. What does this bring up for me?**

   a. *It is difficult to switch from seeing my body as my friend. I have seen it as my enemy for so long that it takes effort for me to make this change.*
   b. *I never thought of my body as a friend. I think this will be helpful to me. It may take some time for me to make this change.*
   c. *Wow! I can have my body work for me instead of against me.*

6

8. What changes in my thinking can I make?

   a. *My body can not respond to me if I don't acknowledge it.*
   b. *Without my body, there would not be me. Therefore,
   I can try to make this a meaningful, rather than a
   destructive, relationship.*
   c. *It takes more energy to hate my body than to love it.*
   d. *Appreciate what my body can do instead of how it looks.*

**9. What are my fears in developing a positive relationship with
   my body?**

   a. *I am afraid that if I love my body, I will become self-
   centered and egocentric.*
   (Where did you learn this to be a cause and effect situation?)

   b. *I am afraid I will appear snotty and act as if I am better
   than others.*
   (Loving your body doesn't mean you have to change
   your personality.

   c. *I am afraid if I like my body and I no longer want to abuse
   it, I could not eat the junk food that I love.*
   (Perhaps you then would not crave the junk food because
   your junk food habit may be a way of punishing yourself.)

10. Beliefs that I have that keep me from accepting my body today:

   a. *Unless my body is perfect, I cannot accept it.*
   (Having a perfect body as a goal can be a terrible trap since
   it makes you feel inadequate.)

   b. *If I accept it, I will not change to make it like I want it to be.*
   (The opposite may be true.)

   c. *In order to change my body, I have to keep beating and
   abusing it.*
   (Is it working for you to do this?)

11. Beliefs I can change about my body include:

   a. *I can tell myself I love my body.*
      (Fake it until you make it.)

   b. *I can love my body without it being perfect.*
      (Striving for a perfect body is an unrealistic goal.)

   c. *I can accept and love my body even if it is not at the*
      ideal weight.
      (Loving your body is a step in reaching your ideal weight.)

EXERCISES:

1. *Describe your experience of being a baby, child, adolescent, and adult. What changes in your body and body image have taken place at each of these times in your life? Can you pinpoint the period in your life when you began to feel negative about your body?

2. *Look at yourself in the mirror, seeing yourself as others see you. Do not judge and do not criticize yourself. Say nice things about yourself as you look into the mirror. Continue to look in the mirror until you believe what you say.

3. *Look at or imagine your family at a reunion. How are you similar and different from others in your family? What is the weight of the males versus females in your family?

4. Write down ten words that describe your negative feelings and attitudes about your body. Allow yourself to experience fully what it means for you to identify yourself this way. Now let go of this self-identification as if you were taking off your clothes. Replace it with a healthy image. On a scale of 1-10, how does it feel to let go of your negative attitudes toward your body? (1= feels awful; 10= feels great.)

5. Visualize yourself accepting your body today. Remember to start with one part of your body at a time. Close your eyes and get in a peaceful state of mind. Relax and begin to get in touch with your

body. How does your body feel? Your head? Your shoulders? Your arms? Your breasts? Your stomach? Your legs? Your feet?

6. For additional help, read Transforming Your Body Image by Marcia Hutchinson. (*Reprinted with permission by Marcia Germaine Hutchinson. © 1985. Published by the Crossing Press: Freedom, CA.). Other books which may be helpful to you are When Women Stop Hating Their Bodies by Hirschman and Munter, One Size Does Not Fit All by Beverly Naidus, or Body Love by Rita Freedman.

"Good bye Fat"

Females with an eating disorder look at their fat differently than people who don't have an eating disorder. Females without an eating disorder look at the fat in their breasts and hips as feminine. Anorexics hate the roundness of their bodies and see this as fatness. Bulimics and binge eaters view their fat as an enemy and want to rid themselves of any fat, no matter what their genetic disposition is. Males view their fat as weakness and representing babyhood. They tend to be especially sensitive to belly weight.

If you want to lose weight, it is important to realize that your fat has served a purpose for you. Reasons people have the need for their fat include the following.

Purposes of Fat

1. POWER:

More weight, more power.
(As one feels more powerful, there is less need for fat.)

2. TO BE NOTICED:

Negative attention is better than no attention.
(Realize that you can be noticed with colorful clothes and striking hair, without having to carry extra weight.)

9

3. SAFETY FROM SEXUAL FEELINGS:

> *With the extra weight, I don't have to worry about sexual attacks, being promiscuous or unfaithful to my partner.*

4. PROTECTION:

> *The heavier I am, the more protected my heart is from being vulnerable or hurt again.*

In order to let go of your fat, you must first find other ways to fulfill the need the fat provides. It is interesting to watch my clients find other ways than their fat to provide power, protect themselves and to feel comfortable with their sexual feelings. Until you do this, however, it is difficult to make the change to let go of the fat. I remember one client who said that once she had become more comfortable with her sexual feelings, she had the following dialogue with her fat.

Client:	*Fat, you have been around for a very long time. You have served me well. You have been there as a cushion to protect me from some of the hurtful things others have said to me. You have cushioned my heart so that I did not get hurt. You have allowed me a lot of protection.*
Fat:	*Yes, I did do all those things for you. However, I also was a burden to you. I made you tired. It was hard work for you to carry me around with you all the time. It was also because of me that you were laughed at and needed me to protect you from that laughter.*
Client:	*Yes, that is true. You know, I am feeling that I don't need you any longer to protect me. I have learned new skills, but you have been with me for so long that it is hard to say good bye and to let you go.*
Fat:	*But, I am ready to go and have been for some time. I feel you do not need me like you once did.*
Client:	*I agree, but I feel sad to say, "Good bye fat."*

Fat: *I know. I will miss you too, but with every ending is a new beginning and I wish you well without me.*

Client: *Thank you. I appreciate that.*

SELF EVALUATION:

1. Purposes my fat has served:

   a. *Lack of fat gets me a lot of attention. (Anorexic)*
   b. *Keeps me from being promiscuous. (Bulimic)*
   c. *Keeps me from getting hurt and abused. (Binge eater)*

2. Fears of letting go of my fat:

   a. *I can't protect myself from pain and hurt without my fat.*
   b. *I will feel lost because it has been a part of me for so long.*
   c. *I will lose my fat and it will come back with even more fat.*

3. Advantages of letting go of my fat:

   a. *I will feel better and lighter.*
   b. *I will be less discriminated against.*
   c. *I can do more things, such as exercise without hurting.*
   d. *I will be healthier.*

4. Beliefs that I have regarding my thinness or my fatness:

   a. *My thinness is what makes others like me. (Anorexic)*
      (Do you chose friends according to how much they weigh? I doubt it. So why do you think others would like you because of your size?)

   b. *My fatness protects me from being hurt. (Bulimic and binge eater)*
      (What other ways can you protect yourself?)

   c. *My thinness is the only part of my life which I am able to control. (Anorexic)*

11

5. Beliefs that I could replace the thoughts mentioned above:

    a. *People do not judge my worth according to how thin I am. Instead, they judge me on the type of person I am. (Anorexic)*

    b. *I can gain control in other aspects of my life so that I don't have to have so much control with my eating. (Anorexic)*

    c. *I can protect myself by asserting myself. (Bulimic and binge eater)*

6. Action I could take regarding my fatness:

    a. *Be realistic about what I should weigh according to my past and family genetics.*

    b. *Lose fat slowly by eating healthy and exercising.*

    c. *Love my body today no matter what my size.*

7. My eating and weight is related to my fatness by:

    a. *The more I obsess about my eating, the more I starve myself. (Anorexic)*

    b. *The more I obsess about my fat, the more I purge. (Bulimic)*

    c. *The more I make negative statements about my fat, the more I overeat. (Binge eater)*

EXERCISES:

1. Visualize yourself letting go of undesirable fat. On a scale of 1-10, how does it feel to no longer have your excess fat?

2. Have a dialogue with your fat. What do you need to say to your fat? What does your fat need to say to you?

3. Journal about your feelings and thoughts related to your fat.

4. For additional help, read Am I Fat? Helping Young Children Accept Differences in Size by Ikedaand Naworski, Appearance Obsession: Learning to Love the Way You Look by Joni E. Jonston, Fat and Furious by Judi Hollis, or Fat is a Feminist Issue I & 11 by Susie Orbach.

12

Medical Problems

If you suffer from anorexia nervosa, it is important to look at the health aspects of your illness. Starving yourself is harmful to your body. It can lead to dehydration and disturbances in the body's fluid/mineral balance causing irregular heartbeat, a heart attack, kidney failure, as well as irreversible liver damage, diabetes and hypoglycemia. Severe hypoglycemia has a poor prognosis. It is often associated with sudden death. Mortality is 10 to 20 percent and no more than 50 percent recover. To determine if you or someone you love is anorexic, look for the following symptoms.

Anorexic's Physical Symptoms

1. Excessive weight loss. (15 percent)
2. Dry thin hair.
3. Dry skin covered with downy fuzz.
4. Brittle splitting nails.
5. Weak and wasted muscles or tremors.
6. Constipation, bloating and abdominal discomfort.
7. Kidney and bladder infections.
8. Urinary tract stones.
9. Cavities and gum disease
10. Frantic activity alternating with lethargy and depression.
11. Amenorrhea, the absence of three or more consecutive menstrual cycles.

Because a male anorexic does not have a loss of a period as a symptom, it is common to misdiagnose or overlook the male anorexic. Male anorexics have a decreased testosterone level and often a decreased libido. Men with medical and health problems tend to be overly sensitive to eating disorders.

Bulimics may throw up after eating, use laxatives, diuretics, enemas, or excessive exercise to try to maintain their weight. If you use syrup of ipecac, STOP IMMEDIATELY. It can quickly cause a toxic reaction to the heart that results in death. Karen Carpenter's death was a result of ipecac toxicity. Prognosis is better for bulimics than anorexics and more than 80 percent of bulimic patients recover. Bulimia is more common than anorexia, affecting at least 3 percent to 10 percent of adolescent and college-age women in the United States.

Physical Symptoms of
the Bulimic and Binge Eater

1. Weight changes because of alternating diets and binges.
2. Menstrual irregularities.
3. Swollen glands in neck beneath jaw.
4. Sore throats or sinus infections.
5. Hair loss.
6. Cavities and loss of tooth enamel.
7. Weak muscles.
8. Puffy, splotched face.
9. Raw fingers from acid from vomiting. (Russell's sign)
10. Bags under eyes.
11. Fainting spells.
12. Blurred vision.
13. Tremors.
14. Rapid or irregular heartbeat.
15. Stomach and abdominal discomfort as well as bloating.
16. Nausea.
17. Edema. (Water retention)
18. Ulcers or colitis.
19. Blood sugar irregularities.
20. Kidney and bladder infections.
21. Weak muscles.

Gorging and forced vomiting can rupture the stomach or esophagus and can cause massive infections and death. If the esophagus does rupture, it is a true medical emergency. Heart attacks, irregular heartbeat, kidney failure, and irreversible liver damage may result. "Chipmunk cheeks" may be the result of swelling and a direct result of binge eating that involves consuming high caloric foods in large quantities over a short period. Others postulate that chronic regurgitation of acidic gastric contents is responsible. Some believe enzymes brought into the mouth during vomiting stimulate taste receptors. The increased autonomic stimulation causes salivary glands to swell. Others think it is the body preserving food before elimination.

Laxative use promotes dehydration, which gives patients a false sense of having lost weight. Chronic diarrhea, potassium depletion, and laxative dependency can cause the colon to lose its normal peristalsis. Colectomy to treat intractable constipation is sometimes necessary.

If you are a binge eater who engages in binges and consumes a great deal of food, you are at risk for the preceding problems as well. You are also at a high risk for diabetes, hypoglycemia, cancer, heart problems, and intestinal and digestive problems. Think about the wear and tear your obesity has on your organs. They have to work longer and harder with the extra weight, which can cause damage or shut down the organs. "Yo-yo" dieting with weight going up and down appears to be more damaging to your body than obesity, so start to eat the way that you can for the rest of your life. Don't look for a quick fix--there is none.

Whether you are an anorexic, bulimic, or a binge eater, it is important to have your health monitored regularly, especially your electrolyte levels (potassium, chloride, and sodium) because they can change quickly.

The relationship between an eating disorder and depression is high. Until recently, people with an eating disorder refused anti-depressants because a side effect is weight gain. This is all a person who is gaining weight or fearful of gaining weight needs to hear. Fortunately, Prozac, Zoloft, Serzone, or Paxil do not have weight gain as a side effect. In fact, for some, weight loss occurs as well as a decreased obsession with food and decreased need to binge or purge.

One of the most drastic reactions I ever saw was with a client who had tried to stop purging for years. None of the behavioral techniques seemed to be of much help. After a few days of using Prozac, the purging stopped, depression lessened, and she felt and looked like a different person. For most people, the results are much less dramatic and usually take two to four weeks before any change occurs. Many of the clients I see are concerned about their addictive personality and are concerned that they will become addicted to anti-depressants. Fortunately, anti-depressants are not addictive. Some people are able to get off them in six months, although others may need to be on them for their entire life. Again, this is a personal decision and needs to have your physician evaluate its use with you.

Diet pills cause serious side effects that include elevated blood pressure, palpitations, seizures, renal failure, anxiety attacks and intra-cerebral hemorrhage. Stopping the use of diet pills usually results in regaining the lost weight.

SELF EVALUATION:

1. **Medical problems I now have:**
2. **Medical problems that my family has:**
3. **Fears I have regarding my health:**

   a. *I will become fat like my obese mother. (Anorexic)*
      (You will probably will have to work hard to follow an exercise program and healthy eating habits in order to not be obese.)

   b. *My purging will stop regulating my weight. (Bulimic)*
      (The longer you purge, the less effective purging becomes.)

   c. *I will become diabetic because of my obesity. (Binge eater)*
      (There is a greater chance of your becoming diabetic with an increase in weight.)

4. **Beliefs that I have that are related to my health:**

   a. *The less I eat, the happier I am. (Anorexic)*
   b. *Purging allows me to eat whatever I want and not gain weight. (Bulimic)*
   c. *Since I have good health, I do not need to be concerned about my weight or eating habits.*

16

5. **Beliefs that I could have about my health:**

   a. *When I don't eat enough for my body to nurture it, I am doing damage to my body. (Anorexia)*

   b. *Purging is not a healthy way to maintain weight. I know it is dangerous to my health, but right now I don't care. (Bulimic).*

   c. *Even though I may be in good health now, the longer I have poor eating habits, the more likely I will have health problems later.*

6. **Action I could take to have fewer health problems:**

   a. *Identify what my health problems are. Recognize the relationship of my health problem with my eating behavior.*

   b. *Sleep, eat, and exercise more or less, whichever I need to do.*

   c. *Get a physical regularly.*

   d. *Eat less fatty foods.*

7. **My eating and weight are related to my medical problems:**

   a. *My starving myself makes me very tired. (Anorexic)*

   b. *My purging makes me very weak. (Bulimic)*

   c. *My obesity makes me very exhausted and contributes to my diabetes. (Binge eater)*

8. **My reaction and fears about the use of an anti-depressant:**

   a. *I don't have a problem, so why should I use an anti-depressant? (Anorexic)*
      (Not eating is a problem for your health.)

   b. *I am afraid to give up my purging. If I purge I will throw up the medication so it will not do me any good to take it.(Bulimic)*
      (The medication may help lessen your urge to purge.)

   c. *I am afraid I will become addicted to an anti-depressant.*
      (Anti-depressants are not addictive.)

9. **Family history of persons who were on medications for depression or should have been:**

   a. *My mom who cried all the time and often would just stay in bed.*
   b. *My uncle who killed himself.*
   c. *My brother who used alcohol to try to help him forget about his problems. Unfortunately, it only made the depression worse.*

10. **Action I can take to make the best decision about whether I should take an anti-depressant:**

   a. *Talk to my doctor about the pros and cons of taking an anti-depressant.*
   b. *Talk to my doctor about the different types of anti-depressants and the possible side effects of each.*
   c. *Read about anti-depressants so I am more knowledgeable and I can make the best choice for me.*

11. **Action I could take instead of an anti-depressant:**

   a. *Increase my exercise.*
   b. *Decrease my intake of fats and sugars and eat healthy foods.*
   c. *Change my negative thinking.*
   d. *Express my anger rather than turning it inward.*

EXERCISES:

1. Visualize yourself not having the medical problems you now have. On a scale of 1-10, how does this feel? Is there any action you can take to lessen your medical problems? What keeps you from taking this action?

2. Visualize yourself lessening your depression, urge to eat, and obsessive thoughts about food. Visualize yourself no longer bingeing or purging. How does that feel? Remember you can get where you want to be by imagining and visualizing how you want to be.

3. Make a list of family health problems. Indicate action you can take to not get the same problems.

4. For additional help, read <u>Listening to Prozac</u> by Peter Kramer, or <u>Medical Issues and Eating Disorder</u> by Kaplan and Garfinkel.

Exercise and Metabolism

Exercise helps people with eating disorders to appreciate what their bodies can do and to value more than how they look. Exercise is one way people lose weight when they have not changed their eating habits. It increases your metabolism and may result in acting as an appetite depressant. If you don't like to exercise, it is important that you begin with an exercise that is the most enjoyable for you. Start out slowly. As you increase the amount you exercise, you will also want to increase the intensity. Remember that 20-30 minutes, five or six days a week will give you the best results. In addition, two 30-minute periods is better than one hour at a time. The earlier in the day you start your exercising, the more benefit for the rest of the day.

Walking with a friend can be beneficial. If your weight is so high that you are uncomfortable when you walk, you may have better success in water. Many of my clients who are overweight say they are embarrassed to be seen in a bathing suit. I remind them that they are doing this for their body and not to please anyone else. What others think of you is less important than improving your health.

In the early stages of anorexia, anorexics exercise excessively. In the later stages, the anorexic doesn't have the energy to exercise. In fact, many become so ill that they are unable to get out of bed. Some bulimics exercise as a means of purging; most binge eaters do not enjoy exercise.

Characteristics of men who exercise extensively are similar to those of the female anorexics. Men become obsessed with exercising and view their worth according to how much they exercise. It becomes an addiction. Athletic training is how many men first start their eating disorders. Male jockeys, wrestlers, swimmers, and dancers see physical appearance as being vital to their success. This makes them more vulnerable to eating disorders. Males who were wrestlers in high school and college often continue their bulimic trends after they give up the sport.

Benefits of exercising

1. Burns calories.
2. Helps control appetite.
3. Increases metabolic rate.
4. Preserves the body's muscles.
5. Increased exercise increases one's energy level.
6. Helps reduce stress.
7. Improves oxygen intake, muscle mass and bone density, which combats osteoporosis and helps make bones stronger.

There is a wide difference among people in regard to their metabolic rate. Metabolism is the rate at which the body burns calories. Studies have shown that your metabolic rate directly affects your propensity toward obesity or thinness. Although we are born with our own rate of metabolism, we are not powerless to change it. Each of us begins with a natural set point, a weight to which our body naturally gravitates. Heredity, percentage of fat, lean body tissue, and lifestyle habits, which include diet and physical activity, determine our set point. In order to lose weight, the goal is to increase one's metabolism and lower the natural set point.

Ways to increase your metabolism

1. Eat more often.
2. Avoid "yo-yo" dieting.
3. Exercise to increase your metabolism.
4. Eat in a healthy way that you can maintain for the rest of your life.
5. As you get older, your metabolism slows down. Therefore, you will need less food.
6. Eat complex carbohydrates (fruits, vegetables, grains), which metabolize faster than simple carbohydrates (fats and sugars).

SELF EVALUATION:

1. Other benefits I could get from exercising:

   a. I will feel better.
   b. I will look more fit.
   c. Less likely to get diseases.
   d. Be active rather than sitting.

2. Excuses I give for not exercising:

   a. Exercise takes too much time.
   (Even if it makes the difference in how you feel?)

   b. Fearful I will eat more.
   (Exercise may decrease your appetite.)

   c. I am not athletic.
   (You do not have to choose a sport requiring athletic ability.)

3. Type of exercise that I could start which I would most enjoy:

   a. Walking.
   b. Bicycle riding.
   c. Swimming.

4. What could I do instead of over exercising?

   a. Meditate.
   b. Yoga.
   c. Relax.
   d. Read.

5. When I over exercise, it keeps me from thinking about:

   a. All the things I have to get done.
   b. My problems.
   c. My weight.
   d. My ex-husband.

6. **My eating is related to my exercise in that:**

   a. *When I exercise I do not have to eat. (Anorexic)*
   (Your body will not be able to continue to do this for very long. It is dangerous to your health.)

   b. *After exercising, I feel less like purging. (Bulimic)*
   (This is probably the result of serotonin sent to the brain.)

   c. *After exercising, I feel less like bingeing. (Binge eater)*
   (This is true unless you tell yourself that since you exercised, you can eat more.)

   d. *My eating is less out of control if I exercise. (Bulimic and binge eaters)*
   (The better you feel, the less you need to binge.)

7. **Things I do that decrease the speed of my metabolism:**

   a. *Starve myself. (Anorexic)*
   b. *Do not eat until dinnertime. Then I binge and purge.(Bulimic)*
   c. *I do not eat the right combination of food to get the maximum benefit of my metabolism. (Binge eater)*
   d. *I watch television or read rather than being active. (Binge eater)*

EXERCISES:

1. Visualize yourself exercising in the way that is most enjoyable for you. On a scale of 1-10, how does it feel not to exercise? How does your body feel after you exercise?

2. Keep a record of the amount and type of exercise that you do daily. Rate the intensity on a scale of 1-10.

3. For additional help, read Make the Connection by Oprah Winfrey and Bob Greene or Compulsive Exercise and Eating Disorders by Alayne Yates.

Life Style of Healthy Eating

You want to choose a style of eating that you can continue for the rest of your life. Most of us can't be on a restrictive diet forever. Your past experiences will indicate what works for you and what doesn't. I doubt you would be buying this book if you had success with your past eating and dieting habits. The more you can structure your eating of three meals plus one or two snacks daily, the less obsessed you will become with your eating. When you use the food guide pyramid for food choices, it allows you a combination of foods that's healthy for you and can help cut down your cravings for sweets and sugars.

Make sure that you try to normalize your eating pattern over a length of time, rather than changing overnight. It is helpful to label foods as healthy rather than good or bad. When you tell yourself a food is bad, it often triggers overeating and binges. Some people find that artificial sweeteners stimulate their appetite, triggering cravings for sugar.

It is important to limit the amount of fat in your diet. The American Heart Association currently recommends that you get no more than 30 percent of your total calories from fat. Saturated and polyunsaturated fat intake should not exceed 10 percent each, with monounsaturated fat making up the remaining 10-15 percent of fat total calories.

If you are like most Americans, about 37 percent of your calories come from fat. If you cut down on your fat intake, not only will you lose weight, but you will also cut down your risk of heart disease, cancer, diabetes, and many other life-threatening illnesses. If you use drugs and alcohol, it will often increase your desire for high fat foods. The labels on food will tell you the number of calories per serving as well as calories from fat. It is helpful to look at labels to learn the amount of fat in foods you eat.

How to Stop the Deprivation

One of the reasons diets don't work is that no one likes to feel deprived. We only take the feeling of deprivation for so long before we try to compensate by eating more than what we need. You set yourself up for a binge when you deprive yourself. Begin now to think of having plenty rather than deprivation.

You can lose weight without depriving yourself. This concept is one of the harder ones for most people to grasp. They feel deprivation is the only way they can lose weight. You may also feel that because when you haven't deprived yourself you've gained weight. When you think of deprivation instead of abundance, it often causes you to overeat. When there is plenty of water, you don't crave water. When you think there is plenty of food, your cravings lessen. Even if you grew up without enough food and hoarded your share, it doesn't mean you have to eat it all now. The thought that you can eat tomorrow doesn't enter the thoughts of a person during a binge.

I remember how anxious a client felt when her daughter was selling Girl Scout cookies because the client felt she had to eat her share right away. When I suggested she buy herself a year's supply and hide the cookies so she would have plenty, she looked as if she had died and gone to heaven. This has an interesting follow-up. Once she realized that she had a year to eat all the cookies, it took away the urgency of having to eat all of them right away. Grocery stores always have food. You can go back tomorrow when you run out and get more. People with eating disorders have to keep reminding themselves of this concept.

When you think of abundance rather than deprivation, don't think this means that you eat plenty of unhealthy foods. Instead, think in terms of healthy foods. Sometimes you can have unhealthy foods, but if you eat them regularly, they will make you feel bad. To have plenty of healthy food means you will feel better. It will also help you be less obsessive about food. Deprivation makes you obsess and think about food all the time. Often, the guilt of overeating makes you feel you must deprive yourself. How long are you going to deprive and punish yourself? You must change your thoughts from deprivation to plentiful before you can change your eating behaviors successfully.

SELF EVALUATION:

1. My patterns of deprivation include:

    a. *I starve myself. I go all day without eating. (Anorexic)*
    b. *I buy things for the rest of my family but don't buy new things for me. (Bulimic and binge eater)*
    c. *I don't allow myself to eat foods that I enjoy. (Binge eater)*

2. Results of depriving myself include:

    a. I feel in charge. (Anorexic)
    b. It sets me up for a purge. (Bulimic)
    c. Not eating foods I enjoy sets me up to overeat these foods
       when I allow myself to eat them. (Binge eater)

3. My fears of not depriving myself include:

    a. I am afraid if I do not deprive myself, I will get even fatter.
    b. I fear I will never stop eating.
    c. I fear all I would eat is food that is unhealthy for me.
    d. I only know how to deprive myself of nice and healthy
       things. I feel as if I don't deserve to have things.
       (<u>How nice it will feel when you start treating yourself</u>
       <u>the way you deserve to be treated. You will like it.</u>*)*

4. Beliefs that I could change about deprivation vs. plenty:

    a. I don't have to deprive myself in order to be in control.
       (Anorexic)
    b. I can change my belief about deprivation by saying there is
       plenty, and I don't have to eat it all today. (Bulimic and
       binge eater)
    c. Plenty does not mean it has to be unhealthy. (Binge eater)

EXERCISES:

1. Fill a plate full of food, filling it with as much as the plate can hold.
Make it abundant. Now eat this food slowly. You have an abundance
of food and an abundance of time. What feelings does this bring up
for you?

    a. Overwhelmed. (Anorexic)
    b. Surprised that I could do it. I know it is supposed to be what
       I do, but I am not usually successful at eating slowly.
       (Bulimic)
    c. When I ate slower, I didn't have to finish all the food.

2. Write in your journal the ways you deprive yourself. Next to the deprivation indicate the action you can take to stop the deprivation.

3. For additional help, read <u>Living Without Dieting</u> by Foreyt & Goodrick or <u>Breaking Out of Food Jail</u> by Jean Antonello.

Eat When Physically Hungry

Physical hunger is when your body, not your mind, tells you that you need food. When your stomach growls, you may feel shaky or light-headed because your body needs food as fuel. Measure your physical hunger on a scale from 0-6 (see chart below). Train yourself to eat when you are at level 1 and to stop at level 4. Description of these levels follows.

Physical Hunger Scale

0=Shaky, light-headed. Feel as if you are going to pass out. For most it has been 6-7 hours since you last ate.
1=Stomach growling, healthy food sounds better to you than sweets. For most it has been 3-4 hours since last ate.
2=Comfortable, could eat, but stomach is not growling. Beginning to feel hungry. For most it has been 2-3 hours since since you last ate. Snack would be appropriate.
3=Food sounds good, but your body does not indicate hunger. This is when you eat for emotional reasons rather than physical reasons, usually 1-2 hours after you've eaten.
4=Eating. Comfortable level. Body is no longer hungry. No longer need additional food. Good time to stop eating.
5=Eating. Feeling full, but that dessert sounds so good. You eat it, but feel uncomfortable afterwards.
6=Eating. Very uncomfortable. Stuffed feeling. Want to just sleep or do nothing because you're too full. It is like you feel after eating a Thanksgiving dinner.

Use the physical hunger chart to measure your physical hunger before and after eating.

Physical Hunger Chart

	Breakfast	Snack	Lunch	Snack	Dinner
Physical hunger before eating	*1*	*3*	*1*	*2*	*1*
Physical hunger after eating	*4*	*4*	*5*	*5*	*4*

Learn to recognize your stomach's hunger signals. Make a conscious effort to tune in to them. Feed your physical hunger by eating foods that you truly enjoy and ones that are healthy for you. Eat when you are hungry and stop before you are full. (Remember, when you stop before you are full, the sooner you will become hungry and the sooner you get to eat again.) Learn to listen to your "full" signals. Take a few bites and stop eating. If you are still hungry, take a few more bites. Again, evaluate if you are hungry.

When listening to your body, ask it what it is hungry for. Is it hungry for spicy, hot, cold, textured, smooth, or comforting food? Don't worry that you will only crave formerly forbidden foods. When you are physically hungry, you will crave what your body needs. Don't worry about occasional setbacks. Don't panic if you binge. Your binge is a sign of anxiety. You also want to replace an old habit with a new one. It takes time for it to feel natural. Many of my clients have said that they don't know when they're hungry or full. This is because they have separated their bodies from their minds. Others have abused these clients' bodies, and in turn, they abuse their bodies with food, not realizing what they are doing. It is easier to pretend not to have a body than to recognize and feel its pain. The first step to stop abusing your body is to recognize when you are hungry and when you are full. Some clients have been able to lose weight simply by changing their eating habits to only eat when physically hungry and stopping before they are full.

EXERCISES:

1. Visualize yourself eating when hungry and stopping when full. Practice until it becomes habit. On a scale of 1-10, how does this feel?

2. Keep a journal of what level of hunger you are at when you eat. Also, indicate how full you are when you stop.

3. For additional help, read <u>Breaking free From Compulsive Eating</u> by Geneen Roth, <u>Intuitive Eating: Recovery Book for the Chronic Dieter</u> by Tribole and Resch, or <u>Thin Within</u> by Judy Wardell.

Break the Destructive Habits and Addictions

Addiction is an activity or behavior that continues although you know it is harmful to you. The feeling of addiction is a sense of urgency, a deep need to fill an empty space inside or an emotional need that represents a connection to another person. An addiction makes you rigid, unreasonably irritable, and unyielding.

Food addiction is similar to alcohol addiction. You may be addicted to sugar as much as an alcoholic is addicted to alcohol. In fact, it is the belief of many that the sugar in alcohol makes alcohol more addictive. The more sugar you eat, the more you crave it. It is common for you to go through a withdrawal period when you stop eating sugar. Withdrawal symptoms may include headaches, shaking, depression, and lack of energy. The symptoms are worst the first three days, but most disappear in a week or two. The best way to lessen the craving for sugar or sweets is to eat many natural sugars in fruits, vegetables, grains, and making sure you have a balance of food from the different food groups.

People with eating disorders often come from alcoholic families or have had previous problems with drugs or alcohol. Many of my patients who were former drug or alcohol addicts indicate their food addiction to be the most difficult to deal with because they can't eliminate food from their diet as they could eliminate drugs or alcohol.

Anorexics often use alcohol in order to give themselves permission to eat. They say that the alcohol helps them to be less obsessive in their thinking. It is often the only time they feel a relief from the restrictions they put on themselves. Bulimic and binge eaters often lose control of their eating when they drink. Most find that they crave salty foods and junk food when drinking or smoking pot.

Depression is also high with alcohol and food addicts. They often turn to drugs or food to make them feel better when it only makes them more depressed. If you are using drugs or alcohol, it is important to stop using them before attempting to conquer your food addiction. Your drinking or drugging does not allow you to have the full mental capacity you need to take care of your food problem.

Many of our eating habits are difficult to break because we have done them for so long. Sometimes we do them because they're the only things we know. Other times it feels so good to do what we are doing, such as snacking all day, that we don't want to change. Decide which habits would be helpful for you to change. Choose one habit in which you can succeed. When you've mastered this, begin working on another habit. Don't overwhelm yourself by trying to change too many habits at once. You are more than likely to fail. Remember, success breeds success. The longer you have had the habit, the harder it is to break. Remember you can replace an old habit with a new one. Most habits take a year before they become automatic and you no longer have to work at changing.

Habits to Change

1. Alcohol consumption.
2. Drink whole milk instead of skim milk.
3. Eat for emotional reasons rather than physical needs.
4. Eat large meals instead of smaller meals.
5. Skip meals.
6. Eat fast without chewing the food slowly.
7. Eat fatty and sweet foods instead of complex carbohydrates.
8. Eat an unbalanced diet.
9. Weigh daily.
10. Eat in the car.
11. Eat standing instead of at a table.
12. Drink coffee and soft drinks instead of water.
13. Watch television instead of exercising.

SELF EVALUATION:

1. **Name family members that have had a drug or alcohol problem.**
2. **What were the actions that family members took to overcome their addiction that you could use for your addictions?**

   a. *Attend Overeaters Anonymous.*
   b. *Get a sponsor.*
   c. *Ask for help from others who have gotten better with their addictions.*

3. **Write those habits you wish to break. How long have you had the habit?**

   a. *Eating fast. My whole family ate fast.*
   b. *Eating when I am not hungry ever since my pregnancy.*
   c. *Not eating balanced meals.*

4. **Where did I learn these habits? What would the people who taught me these habits think if I changed these habits?**

5. **What action can I take to change these habits?**

EXERCISES:

1. Visualize yourself without drugs, alcohol, or a food addiction. On a scale of 1-10, how does it feel without your addiction?

2. Visualize yourself breaking the habit that you have chosen to stop. On a scale of 1-10, how does it feel to continue the habit? Change the habit?

3. Write in your journal the habits that you wish to change. First, list the bad habits. Then choose a habit to start. Keep a record of your progress.

4. For additional help, read <u>Recoveries: True Stories by People Who Conquered Addictions and Compulsions</u> and <u>Dear Kids of Alcoholics</u> by Hall and Cohen.

Trigger Foods

Trigger foods are foods that when you eat a little, they make you want a lot. It is important to distinguish which foods are physiological or emotional triggers for you. If you have physiological reaction to a particular food, you may have an allergic reaction to the food. Your cravings may indicate an allergy to that particular food. It may be a psychological trigger when you crave a food because you don't allow yourself to have it. By denying yourself food, you make it more desirous to you. Rather than saying you can't have certain foods, you may want to change your approach. Ask yourself whether that food is healthy for you. When you allow yourself a choice in what you eat, you feel more in control of your eating.

It is helpful to think ahead about how you will feel after eating a particular food. When you are physically hungry, it is important to ask your body what food you need. When you learn to listen to your body, it can help you make better choices. It is important to be conscious of your food when you eat. This means eliminate all distractions when you eat such as when you are watching TV, driving, cooking, or washing the dishes. When you are conscious of your food and the way it tastes, you will eat slower, chew your food, and enjoy the eating process more than if you inhaled it.

SELF EVALUATION:

1. Name the changes I need to make for the rest of my life.

> *a. I need to eat slower.*
> *b. I need more protein.*
> *c. I need less sugars and fat.*

2. What has and has not worked for me in the past?

> *a. When I ate three meals plus a snack and followed a food plan, I didn't have to be so obsessed about my eating.*
> *b. When I ate slowly and at the table, I was more conscious of my food and ate less.*
> *c. When I ate fruits, I didn't crave as many sweets.*

3. **Name the trigger foods for me. Decide if they are the result of physiological or psychological reaction.**

   a. *Chocolate, desserts, and nuts are my trigger foods. They are physiological in that when I eat them, the more I crave them. When I stop eating them, the craving lessens.*
   b. *They are psychological in that I tell myself I can't have these foods, which only makes me want them more.*

4. **Action I can take to not have these foods be a problem for me:**

   a. *I need to change my thoughts and not beat myself when I have eaten them so that it doesn't set me up for a binge.*
   b. *Introduce them into my pattern of eating slowly, one food at a time.*
   c. *Think of these foods as healthy instead of good or bad foods.*

EXERCISES:

1. Visualize yourself eating, as you will for the rest of your life. On a scale of 1-10, how does it feel to eat as you now do? How does it feel to have a life style of eating?

2. Write your thoughts and feelings about a life style of eating in your journal.

3. For additional help, read <u>Breaking Free from Compulsive Eating</u> by Geneen Roth or <u>Making Peace with Food: Freeing Yourself from the Diet-Weight Obsession</u> by Susan Kano.

How to Stop the Bingeing

Bingeing is most often a result of deprivation. When you think you can't have a particular food or that you have to limit it, it only makes you rebellious. It sets you up to prove you can eat whatever you want and the volume you choose. When you do not eat enough and skip meals, bingeing often results. Skipping meals lets you believe that you have been so good that you deserve to eat more. The hunger that results sets you up to eat more and faster.

To stop bingeing, begin by eating three meals and one or two snacks each day. It takes less control to eat this often than to not allow yourself to eat. Therefore, you don't lose control and binge. Listen to your body. Eat when you are hungry and stop when you are full. You then don't have to measure how much is enough or too much. Your body tells you how much you need. Once you give yourself permission to eat, you no longer have to fight the deprived feelings of not having enough. Choose healthy foods and combinations from the pyramid food groups. Eating the right types of foods and combination of foods reduces the desire to binge because your body is getting what it needs and wants. Most people go through four stages to eliminate bingeing from their life.

Four Stages to Eliminate Bingeing

1. Evaluate what happened to cause the binge. (This is done after a binge.)
2. You realize in the middle of the binge why you are bingeing, but you can't stop.
3. You are able to stop yourself from bingeing during a binge, but not able to stop your binge from starting.
4. Awareness of what causes the binge and you prevent the binge from occurring. (See Binge Diary)

SELF EVALUATION:

1. Evaluate my last binge without judging myself. What was I doing? Thinking? Feeling?

   a. *I was cleaning the house while my husband was watching TV.*
   b. *I was thinking how nice it would be to be able to relax and watch television like my husband was doing.*
   c. *I was angry that he was not helping me with the chores.*
   d. *I hate the fact he thinks his only responsibility is to bring in the income.*

2. **What did I learn from this binge that can be helpful in preventing the next binge?**

   a. *Instead of bingeing, I could tell my husband how I felt.*
   b. *I could ask my husband to help me.*
   c. *I could stop cleaning and join my husband watching TV.*
   d. *I binge in order to not feel.*

3. **What thoughts influenced my binge?**

   a. *I didn't think I had the right to watch television like he was doing.*
   b. *I thought that I should not express my anger.*
   c. *I thought it would be wrong to relax instead of working.*
   d. *I believed it was my duty to do all the housework.*
   e. *It is easier to binge than confront my husband.*

4. **Fears I have if I eliminate my bingeing:**

   a. *I'm afraid I'll have no way to enjoy life.*
   b. *I will become more stressed, since I do not have food to numb me.*
   c. *I'm afraid I will do something more destructive with my free time.*
   d. *I'm afraid I will get too much attention.*
   e. *I'll get bored. I will have lot of time to think.*

5. **Action I can take to not binge:**

   a. *I need to change my thoughts and not beat myself when I have eaten so that it doesn't set me up for a binge.*
   b. *Eat when hungry. Stop when full.*
   c. *Make sure I don't go long periods of time without eating.*
   d. *Follow food guide pyramid to make sure I get the right combination of foods.*
   e. *Eat plenty of fruits, vegetables, and grains so that I don't crave sweets and high fat foods.*
   f. *Change my thinking from deprivation to plenty.*

6. Substitutions for bingeing I could use:

    a. *Delay the binge for a half hour. Tell myself, if I still feel like eating at that time, I will eat.*
       (Often the delay allows you to get distracted and not binge.)

    b. *Write in my diary about what I am feeling in order to prevent the binge.*
       (Since writing gives you a chance to express yourself, you may not have to stuff the feeling with food.)

    c. *Call a friend and talk about what I am feeling.*
       (You can talk to an empty chair and imagine your therapist or friend to be there, even if they are unavailable. This is a great way to be able to work out your problems on your own. When you are able to resolve your own problems, you feel stronger and more self-reliant.)

    d. *Tell myself that bingeing is a choice that I have, but ask how will I feel physically and psychologically if I do binge, and how I will feel if I don't binge.*
       (When you give yourself a choice, you have nothing to rebel against.)

EXERCISES:

1. Visualize yourself not bingeing. Make this happen for you. What feelings does this bring up for you? On a scale of 1-10, how do you feel after bingeing? After stopping a binge?

2. Prior to having your next binge, write in your journal thoughts and feelings you are having. This often interrupts the emergency of the binge.

3. For additional help, read, Overcoming Overeating by Hirshmann & Munter, Overcoming Binge Eating by Christopher Fairburn, or Getting Better Bit(e) by Bit (e) by Schmidt and Treasure.

Binge Diary

DATE	WHAT I ATE	FEELINGS AND THOUGHTS PRIOR TO BINGEING (1-10)	ALTERNATIVES TO BINGEING (1-10)
7/5/98 5:45	7 pieces of fried chicken 3 ears of corn 2 servings of mashed potatoes and gravy 3 rolls 5 pats of butter 1 piece of apple pie ala mode 2 glasses of wine	*I hate my body and myself so I might as well punish my body by overeating.* *(1)*	*Write about how I am angry with myself instead of abusing my body with high fat foods.* *(7)*
7/5/98 9:00	12 beers . 1 bag of chips	*I am so upset with myself. I'll just get drunk. Maybe then I'll feel better.* *(2)*	*Get a movie to watch, read a book, or call a friend.* *(8)*
7/6/98 4:00	1 quart wine 16 oz. package potato chips 1 pizza 5 hot dogs 5 hot dog buns 1 pizza	*I'll just have a glass of wine to help me relax.* *(2)*	*Have a healthy snack. Listen to relaxing music.* *(9)*

How to Stop the Purging

Bulimics use a variety of ways to purge their body of food. The most common way is to stick their fingers down their throat and vomit. Others use laxatives, diuretics, enemas, excessive exercise, or sitting in the sauna for hours. To stop the purging, tell yourself that you are not going to purge even if you binge. For many who purge, not being able to purge helps them not to binge. The statement, "Go ahead and binge because you can get rid of it anyhow" gets them into trouble.

Many bulimics don't realize that the purging doesn't help with weight reduction after a period of time. The longer you purge, the less effective it becomes. Your body starts to slow its metabolism and learns to preserve the food that you eliminate through purging. That is why many bulimics who purge get "chipmunk cheeks." Heat applications to the swollen facial glands or use of tart candies may be helpful to reduce the swelling.

Dental hygiene for bulimics may find rinsing with tap water to feel good, but it may dilute and diminish the buffering capacity of saliva. Similarly, tooth brushing after purging hastens erosion of the weakened enamel. Irreversible changes in your teeth may result due to the purging. The enamel on your teeth will erode. If you have been purging a lot, your stomach will be bloated when you stop. It can be painful, but will stop after a few days. It takes a while for your body to get used to not purging. Some bulimics' hands are raw from purging. Imagine what your throat, stomach, and other vital organs must look like if your hands and teeth are raw.

Review the section in this book on how to stop bingeing because if you can stop bingeing, there is no need to purge. It is dangerous to purge because it becomes automatic to where it is possible to vomit in your sleep and suffocate. The esophagus can also burst, which can result in death. Purging can be a source of relief for you, but there are healthier ways to relax and deal with stress than purging. (See chapter nine-How your stress affects your weight and self-esteem.)

Men who purge tend not to have as much shame about the purging as women. Many times my male bulimics come to see me for reasons other than stopping the bulimic behavior. They tend to indicate that it is no big deal and don't want to deal with it. Their coaches often suggested they use the purging to get at a desired weight. Because their coaches didn't seem concerned, the males shared this attitude.

SELF EVALUATION:

1. When did I begin to purge?

    a. *When my gymnastic coach told me I needed to lose weight.*
    b. *When I lived in the dorm at college and ate high fat foods.*
    c. *When my boyfriend broke up with me because he said I was too fat.*
    d. *When I caught my mom purging.*

2. When do I purge? What sets me up to purge?

    a. *When I starve myself, I set myself up for a binge and purge.*
    b. *When I tell myself I can't have certain foods.*
    c. *I purge when I tell myself I can get rid of the binge by purging.*

3. When do I not need to purge?

    a. *When I am with people and am having a good time.*
    b. *When I have eaten healthily and in small amounts.*
    c. *When I might get caught.*

4. What beliefs could I use to stop purging?

    a. *If I do not allow myself to purge, I will not binge.*
    b. *Purging is bad for my health and can cause me great bodily harm.*
    c. *Purging will cease to be a way to manage my weight after a period of time.*
    d. *I will feel better and have more energy when I stop purging.*

5. What actions or substitutes could I use in place of purging?

    a. *Write my feelings down.*
    b. *Call a friend.*
    c. *Eliminate foods that contribute to my purging until I am able to stop the purging.*

EXERCISES:

1. Recall the last time you purged. Rather than beating yourself up for purging, try to learn from it. Describe what you ate, your feelings and thoughts prior to the purge. (See Purge Diary)

2. Visualize yourself not purging. Practice making this visualization be true for you. On a scale of 1-10, how do you feel when you purge? How would you feel if you stopped purging?

3. Prior to purging, journal your thoughts and feelings. The writing can take the place of bingeing or purging.

4. For additional help, read <u>Bulimia. Guide to Recovery: Understanding and Overcoming the Binge-Purge Cycle</u> by Hall and Cohen, <u>My Name is Caroline</u> by Caroline Miller, <u>The Monster Within. Overcoming Bulimia</u> by Cynthia Rowland, <u>The Bulimic College Student</u> Whitaker and Davis. You may also wish to listen to the tape, <u>Understanding Bulimia</u> by Leigh and Cohn.

Purge Diary

DATE AND TIME	WHAT I ATE	FEELINGS AND THOUGHTS PRIOR TO PURGING (1-10)	ALTERNATIVES TO PURGING (1-10)
9/6/98 7:00 a.m.	1 small orange juice 1 cup coffee	*I am going to be so good today.* *(10)*	*Eat a healthy breakfast so I won't be so hungry.* *(3)*
8:30	3 egg omelet 3 large pancakes 4 sausages 2 toast	*I am so hungry. I'll have something to eat.* *(2)*	*Eat a smaller breakfast and have a snack.* *(8)*

39

DATE AND TIME	WHAT I ATE	FEELINGS AND THOUGHTS PRIOR TO PURGING (1-10)	ALTERNATIVES TO PURGING (1-10)
9/6/98 10:00	2 Snickers candy bar 1 bag potato chips 1 cola drink	*I have already blown my diet, so I might as well have a good binge and purge.* *(8)*	*Have some fruit or a bagel for a snack Take a break and get some fresh air.* *(7)*
1:00	1 large burrito 2 baskets of chips and salsa	*I am going to have a big lunch so I can binge and purge.* *(8)*	*I am going out to lunch with my friends. It is the only part of my job I like.* *(7)*
3:00	1 piece of pie	*I might as well have something else to eat since I have already blown my diet.* *(1)*	*Have a cup of tea or a healthy snack.* *(7)*
5:00	1 hamburger l large fries 1 chocolate malt	*I hate to go home to an empty house and eat alone.* *(2)*	*Wait to eat when I am hungry and stop when I am full.* *(7)*
7:00	1 box of cereal 1 quart of skim milk 1 quart of ice cream 2 candy bars	*I hate myself, my body, and my job. I'll eat to make me feel better.* *(2)*	*Find something fun to do besides eating.* *(8)*

Food Guide Pyramid

The food guide pyramid emphasizes food from the five food groups shown in the three lower sections of the pyramid. Each of these food groups provides some but not all of the nutrients you need. Foods in one group can't replace those in another. One food group is not any more important than another for good health--you need them all. The pyramid is an outline of what to eat each day. It's not a rigid prescription, but a general guide that lets you choose a healthful diet that's right for you. The pyramid calls for eating a variety of foods to get the nutrients you need and at the same time the amount of calories to maintain a healthy weight.

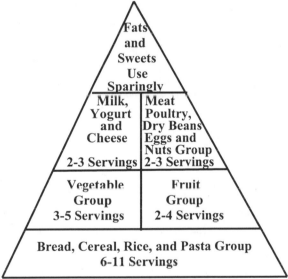

Source: U.S. Dept. of Agriculture and the U.S. Dept. of Health and Human Services

The small tip of the pyramid lists fats and sweets. These include foods such as salad dressings, cream, butter, margarine, sugars, soft drinks, candies, and sweet desserts. Alcoholic beverages are also part of this group. These foods provide calories but few vitamins and minerals. Most people should go easy on foods from this group. Some foods in other food groups may be high in fat and added sugar as well. Consider the fat and added sugars from all the food groups, not just fats and sweets from the pyramid tip.

41

Following Count as 1 serving

1. Bread, Cereal, Rice, and Pasta Group

    a. 1 slice of bread
    b. ½ cup of cooked rice or pasta
    c. ½ cup of cooked cereal or 1 ounce of ready to eat cereal

2. Vegetable Group:

    a. ½ cup of chopped raw or cooked vegetables
    b. 1 cup of leafy raw vegetables

3. Fruit Group

    a. 1 piece of fruit or melon wedge
    b. ¾ cup of juice
    c. ½ cup of canned fruit
    d. ¼ cup of dried fruit

4. Milk, Yogurt, and Cheese Group

    a. 1 cup of milk or yogurt
    b. 1 ½ ounces of natural cheese
    c. 2 ounces of processed cheese

5. Meat, Poultry, Fish, Dry Beans, Eggs and Nuts Group

    a. 2 ½ -3 ounces of cooked lean meat, poultry, or fish.
    b. ½ cup of cooked beans, 1 egg, or 2 Tablespoons of
        peanut butter equals 1 ounce of lean meat.

6. Fats and Sweets
    a. Limit calories from this group.
    b. Don't forget fats from other groups.

Number of Servings Needed

	Women and older adults	Children, teen girls, active women, men	Teen boys and active men
Calorie level	*About 1,600*	*About 2,200*	*About 2,800*
Bread group	*6*	*9*	*11*
Vegetable group	*3*	*4*	*5*
Fruit group	*2*	*3*	*4*
Milk group	*2-3*	*2-3*	*2-3*
Meat group	*2* *Total of 5 oz.*	*2* *Total of 6 oz.*	*3* *Total of 7 oz.*

If you are out of control with your eating, it may be helpful to chart what you are eating to help you gain some control. The top chart asks you to write down the food you eat daily. (An example is given.) The tally chart suggests you mark the category of food for the week. By eating from the different food groups, you will be getting the best combination of your necessary nutrients. This often helps to lessen the craving for unhealthy foods. Following is an example of the minimum daily requirements for each of the food groups.

Food Diary

FOOD GROUP	BREAKFAST	LUNCH	SNACK	DINNER
Bread, Cereal Rice and Pasta (6-11 servings)	*1 c. Bran Flakes* (2 servings)	*2 slices bread* (2 servings)		*1 c. rice* (2 servings)
Vegetables (3-5 Servings)		*1 c. lettuce 1 carrot* (2 servings)		*½ cup broccoli* (1 serving)
Fruits (2-4 servings)	*¾ c. orange juice* (1 serving)		*peach* (1 serving)	
Milk, Yogurt and Cheese (2-3 Servings)	*1 cup milk* (1 serving)			*1 cup milk* (1 serving)
Meat, Poultry, Dry Beans , Eggs and Nuts (2-3 servings)		*1 ounce turkey* (1 serving)		*2 ounces salmon* (1 serving)
Fat and Sweets (Use sparingly)		*1 tsp. mayonnaise*		

After writing what you eat each day, it is helpful to tally the food groups to see that you have the recommended number.

Tally

	Mon	Tues	Wed	Thur	Fri	Sat	Sun
Bread Group	*llllll* 6	*6*	*6*	*6*	*7*	*6*	*7*
Vegetables	*llll* 4	*3*	*5*	*4*	*4*	*3*	*3*
Fruit	*ll* 2	*3*	*2*	*4*	*3*	*3*	*2*
Milk Group	*lll* 3	*2*	*2*	*3*	*2*	*2*	*2*
Meat Group	*ll* 2	*2*	*3*	*2*	*2*	*3*	*2*

To figure how many calories you can eat and still lose an average of one pound a week, multiply your current weight by 10. (This formula estimates a calorie reduction to lose 25 pounds or more.)

Current weight in pounds_____ x 10 +_____ calories

You can use this calorie level as your daily target. If you've figured you need 1,400 calories, follow the pyramid food guide. If your daily target is less than 1,400 calories, increase your activity to burn more calories. Eating fewer calories boosts your chances for running short of necessary nutrients.

The basic menu has about 55 percent from carbohydrates, 20-25 percent from protein, and 25-30 percent from fat. Each day, plan your meals using the suggested servings from each food group.

If your daily target exceeds 1,400 calories, use this guide:

1,500 calories--add 1 bread serving
1,600 calories--add 1 bread, l meat, 1 fat
1,700 calories--add 2 bread, 1 meat, 1 fat
1,800 calories--add 2 bread, 1 fruit, 2 meat, 1 fat
1,900 calories--add 2 bread, 1 vegetable, 1 fruit, 2 meat, 2 fat
2,000 calories--add 2 bread, 1 vegetable, 1 fruit, 2 meat, 1 milk, 2 fat

Healthy Alternatives to Bingeing

It is important when you begin to change your eating habits to have some alternatives available besides eating to fulfill your needs. It is automatic at this point for you to turn to food to make you feel good. It may be helpful to make a list of your needs. Then indicate how you can meet these needs in other ways. Place this list on the refrigerator. When you reach for food, look at your list and choose one of the alternatives instead. Some of my clients have found it helpful to take a jar and place different alternatives to food in the jar. When they want to turn to food, they take an alternative out of the jar and do what the note says instead of eating. This may not be necessary later, but it can be helpful to help you begin to change your eating habits. Identify your needs and use alternatives to eating.

Alternatives

NEEDS	ALTERNATIVES
Boredom: Need for an activity instead of eating.	
	Watch TV, a video or listen to music.
	Do relaxation techniques.
	Start a new hobby.
	Take some classes.

46

Overwhelming Feelings (Anger, Sadness, Anxiety)	
	Check out my irrational thoughts.
	Talk about what's bothering me.
	Comfort myself.
	Have compassion for myself.
	When feelings are overwhelming, talk myself through the feelings.
	Call a friend.
	Write in my journal about my feelings.
	Accept all my feeling.
	Express my feelings appropriately.
Cause for Celebration	
	Reward myself in ways besides food.
	Invite friends over. Have a party.
	Have fun.
	Do something I've wanted to do, but didn't have time to do.
	Do something nice for the less fortunate.
Stress: Need for relaxation, outlet for stress	
	Exercise.
	Do relaxation techniques.
	Change my negative thinking to affirming thoughts.
	Play, have fun and laugh.
	Limit hours at work.
	Call a friend and talk about my stress.
	Do yoga or deep breathing.
	Watch television.
	Read a book.
	Shop.

Physical Evaluation

BEHAVIOR	USUAL PRACTICE (1-10)	ACTION TO TAKE (1-10)
Breakfast	*Skip breakfast.* *(4)*	*Eat breakfast to speed up my metabolism.* *(6)*
Snack in morning, afternoon, and evening	*I don't snack between meals.* *(4)*	*Have a healthy snack so that I am not so starved for meals.* *(7)*
Lunch	*Have a large lunch.* *(4)*	*Have a healthy lunch.* *(7)*
Vegetables	*Eat very little. Do not like vegetables.* *(3)*	*Eat vegetables raw instead of cooked ones.* *(7)*
Protein foods	*I do not get enough protein in my diet.* *(3)*	*Add protein drinks to get the necessary protein.* *(6)*
Sugar	*I love sugar, but I feel bad when I eat it.* *(1)*	*Eat more fruits to get natural sugar.* *(7)*

BEHAVIOR	USUAL PRACTICE (1-10)	ACTION TO TAKE (1-10)
Speed eating	*I eat too fast.* *(2)*	*Give myself time to chew and enjoy the food.* *(8)*
Bingeing	*I binge all day and night.* *(1)*	*Eat 3 meals and 2 snacks to lessen my binges.* *(7)*
Purging	*I purge after I eat anything.* *(1)*	*Tell myself I am not going to binge to lessen the need to purge.* *(8)*
Body image	*I hate my body.* *(1)*	*Start saying "I love my body" until I believe it.* *(8)*
Awareness of my body.	*Unaware of what my body needs.* *(2)*	*Listen and talk to my body to find out what it needs.* *(8)*
Drugs, Alcohol	*Use daily.* *(2)*	*Discontinue use.* *(7)*
Exercise	*Hate it.* *(1)*	*Start slowly.* *(7)*

CHAPTER TWO

Change Your Thoughts to Change Your Weight and Self-esteem

*O*ur intellectual self is as much of who we are as is our weight or physical appearance. We often take our mind for granted without appreciating what our minds are capable of doing. Our minds allow us to be creative and to change our thinking so that we can change our behaviors and how we feel. Most often our feelings are ruled by what we think. Learning to think in a way that is healthy for us is a large part of what we need to do to overcome our eating problems.

Most anorexics appear to be very bright. Because of their perfectionism, anorexics are often the valedictorian or at the top of their class, have very high grades, and present themselves as "good girls." Yet, because of the energy they use in their eating disorder, they are not using their maximum ability in their intellectual pursuits. Since they limit their thinking as to what they deem acceptable, they often take few risks and are not very creative in their thinking. They see things in black-or-white, perceiving extremes without awareness of gray areas. It is either all good or all bad and there is nothing in-between. This causes much distress for them and others around them. This thinking does not allow for flexibility, causing them to be looked on as self-centered. To the anorexic, it is their survival tool to be in control.

■■■

Bulimic and binge eaters may be more creative and flexible than anorexics, but they also are unable to use their potential because of the amount of thinking and energy they use purging or bingeing. When you realize the amount of time that you spend thinking about food, there is little time left to think about the other aspects of your life. When you change your beliefs, you are then free to change your behaviors. Becoming aware of what beliefs you have that interfere with changing your eating habits is important in order for you to overcome your problem.

How to Change Your Stinking Thinking

The following are examples of thinking patterns people with eating disorders often have. If you think in any one of the following ways, it will affect how you feel about yourself. The more stinking your thinking, the worse you will feel. Changing your thinking will change how you feel. Think of examples when you use the following types of thoughts and then change that thought.

1. **PERFECT THINKING. You look at things in black and white without seeing grays.**

    a. *If I eat one cookie, I might as well eat the whole bag.*
    b. *If I come in second place, I might as well have come in last.*
    c. *I must either go on a diet or eat everything in sight.*
    d. *I must have a perfect body or my body is unacceptable.*

2. **DEDUCTIVE REASONING. You deduct that a negative statement or experience is the complete truth.**

    a. *Because my boyfriend thinks I am fat, everybody thinks I am fat.*
    b. *Because I gained a pound this week, I am going to gain twenty pounds this month.*
    c. *Because I purged once last month, I am never going to be able to stop the purging.*
    d *Because my mom is morbidly obese, there is nothing I can do to prevent my being obese.*

52

3. SCREEN THOUGHTS. You screen what you allow to enter your thoughts.

   a. *Your boss gave you a suggestion of how you could improve.*
       (You forget the praise she gave you.)

   b. *Your friend said she loves being with you and you are a lot of fun, but that she wished you would stop swearing.*
       (All you hear is that she doesn't like you.)

   c. *You receive compliments about how pretty you are, but you think the compliments are just to make you feel better.*
       (You don't feel you are worthy of compliments.)

4. DEVALUE YOURSELF. You put yourself down.

   a. *Oh well, anyone could win that award.*
   b. *Even though I have a pretty face, my hips are too large.*
   c. *No one will want to hire me because I am fat.*

5. NEGATIVE THOUGHTS. You assume the worst.

   a. *When I walk into a room, I am sure everyone is looking at and judging me.*
   b. *I go to an Overeaters Anonymous meeting and everyone there is overweight so I decide O.A. is not working.*
   c. *I am very tired after eating a piece of cake, so I conclude that I am diabetic.*

6. INFLATE OR DEFLATE. You make a thought to be either more or less important than what the reality is.

   a. *Each day I do not exercise, I gain weight because one time I did.*
   b. *If I eat one bite of ice cream, I know I will eat the whole gallon.*
   c. *My last physical indicated that my electrolytes were O.K., so I don't have to worry about my health.*

7. **INTUITIVE REASONING.** **You allow your gut feelings to rule your brain.**

   a. *I have an intuition that I will always be fat so I might as well enjoy eating anything I want.*
   b. *My gut feeling is that my husband's reaction to me must mean he is having an affair.*
   c. *I feel as if I am going to die young, so I am going to eat as if there is no tomorrow.*

8. **VICTIMIZATION STATEMENTS.** **You criticize yourself with shoulds. You feel you have no choices and it make you feel helpless or victimized.**

   a. *I should lose weight and go on a diet.*
   b. *I ought to exercise.*
   c. *I should join a group to get support for my weight issues.*
   d. *I should eat fruits and vegetables instead of high fat foods.*
   e. *I should be more sensitive to others.*

9. **JUDGEMENT.** **You judge yourself negatively.**

   a. *Instead of saying I made a mistake, I call myself stupid.*
   b. *Instead of saying I gained five pounds, I call myself fatso.*
   c. *I think that because I threw up, I am vulgar.*
   d. *I am too fat.*

10. **IRRESPONSIBLE THOUGHTS.** **You feel responsible for others or blame others instead of taking responsibility for your actions.**

    a. *If my mother had not made us clean our plates, I would not have an eating disorder today.*
    b. *If my father had not sexually abused me, I would not be obese today.*
    c. *If my husband had not had an affair, I would not be sad.*
    d. *It is my parents' fault that I am fat.*

EXERCISES:

1. What were you thinking the last time you binged or purged? What was your stinking thinking? What could you have said instead so that you wouldn't have needed to binge or purge?

2. Give examples of when you used stinking thinking. How do you feel about yourself when you think this way? Rate the feeling from 1-10. Now replace the stinking thinking with rational thoughts. Rate yourself from 1-10. See how much better you feel.

3. For additional help, read David Burn's Feeling Good: The New Mood Therapy.

Stinking Thinking

STINKING THINKING	USUAL PATTERN (1-10)	ACTION TO TAKE (1-10)
Perfect Thinking	I see everything as black or white and no grays. (2)	Allow myself not to always see things in extremes. (7)
Deductive Reasoning	I see one negative event as the absolute truth. (2)	See one negative aspect without generalizing it to the entire truth. (8)
Screen Thoughts	Always look at the negative and don't let the positive enter. (2)	Allow positive statements to enter in my beliefs. (9)

STINKING THINKING	USUAL PATTERN (1-10)	ACTION TO TAKE (1-10)
Negative Thoughts	*I always assume the worst.* *(2)*	*Make sure I get all the facts before making assumptions.* *(8)*
Inflate or Deflate Statements	*If it is negative, I make it important. If it is positive, I make it unimportant.* *(2)*	*Value the positive as much if not more than the negative.* *(8)*
Victimization Statements	*I feel like I have no choices. I feel like a victim.* *(1)*	*Ask myself what I want and give myself choices.* *(8)*
Intuitive Reasoning	*Use my intuition rather than my head.* *(1)*	*Get facts rather than using only my intuition.* *(9)*
Irresponsible Thoughts	*I do not look at my responsibility. I blame others.* *(3)*	*Look at my responsibility so I can take action and feel more powerful.* *(9)*
Judgmental Statements	*I am judgmental.* *(1)*	*Learn from my mistakes without judging them.* *(9)*

Thoughts to Change About Your Body and Self

The following are some of the thoughts a number of my clients have which get them in trouble. Which are ones that you also have? Under each thought, write how this thought gets you into trouble and what thought you could make to change it?

1. **Once I lose this weight, my problems will be solved.**

   a. My weight problem may be solved, but there is the problem of how I keep it off.

   b. If my weight was my only problem, I probably wouldn't have an eating problem.

   c. When I have lost weight before, I didn't feel free of problems.

2. **Eating is the only problem I have.**

   a. My problems with work, husband and money will still be present even if I lose the weight I want.

   b. If eating was the only problem I had, I wouldn't have to use food to hide the other problems.

   c. Eating is only the symptom, not the problem.

3. **It is impossible for me to overcome this eating problem because my parents were not there for me.**

   a. How long am I going to blame my parents to avoid taking responsibility for my actions?

   b. If the reason I eat is the need to be parented, then I must learn to parent myself.

   c. When I say something is impossible, I then make it that way.

4. **I have no willpower since I am obese.**

   a. My genes influence my obesity.

   b. My past "yo-yo" dieting influences my obesity.

   c. If my weight were determined by willpower, I would not be obese since I have tried harder than most.

57

5. **All fat people are unhealthy and all thin people are healthy.**

   a. *Anorexics are not healthy.*
   b. *There are fat people who are healthier than some thin people and vice versa.*
   c. *Not all fat people are unhealthy, however, they would be healthier if they were not as heavy.*

6. **What others think of me is more important than what I think.**

   a. *When I think this way I am giving away my power to others.*
   b. *When I think this way I don't allow myself to take action.*
   c. *How do you know for sure what anyone else thinks but you?*

7. **How I look determines who I am.**

   a. *It is a factor but not the whole determinant.*
   b. *As long as I believe this, I discount the other important parts of who I am.*
   c. *This thought contributes to my overeating since I never feel good enough.*

EXERCISES:

1. Make a list of common thoughts you have which make you feel bad about yourself. After each thought, replace it with one that makes you feel good.

2. For additional help, read <u>Body Traps</u> by Judith Rodin.

Change Negative to Positive Thoughts

When you have negative thoughts, write them in the negative statement column. Then turn the negative into a positive statement and write the new, improved thought in the positive statement column.

NEGATIVE STATEMENT	POSITIVE STATEMENT
I don't deserve a treat.	*Yes I do. I'll treat myself to a new suit. I can treat myself in ways other than food.*
I'm alone. Now is my chance to eat a lot.	*I don't have to be alone to eat what I want.*
I'm going to purge until I get to my ideal weight.	*There are healthier ways to lose weight than purging.*
I want to lose weight fast.	*If I lose weight fast, I'll gain it back fast.*
I am going to starve myself.	*When I starve myself, I set myself up for a binge.*
I can't stop thinking about sweets.	*When I think of sweets, replace this thought with another pleasant thought.*
I am so fat and ugly.	*Although I am not at my ideal weight, I am not ugly. My size does not determine my beauty.*
I will never be able to lose 50 pounds.	*Losing weight in a healthy manner takes time. It will happen if I take a small step at a time.*
I don't deserve to be loved because I am fat.	*I deserve to be loved no matter what I weigh.*

EXERCISES:

1. Draw a line down the middle of the paper. List your negative thoughts on the left side of the paper. On the right side of the paper list the positive statement. After you practice this, you will be able to do this in your mind without writing it.

2. Write in your journal. Then go back and underline your positive and negative thoughts with different colored pens. This will give you the opportunity to see your progress of having more positive than negative statements.

3. For additional help, read <u>Feeling Good Handbook</u> by David Burns.

How to Stop Your Obsessive Thoughts

We tend to be obsessed with food when we deny ourselves, or when we are out of control with our eating. Denying ourselves food makes food all the more attractive to us. It takes a lot of control, energy, and obsessing to not eat. Our bodies crave food when we starve ourselves. An anorexic constantly gives food to others because she always thinks about food and since she doesn't allow herself to eat, she wants others to eat. This allows her to have a better sense of control when she doesn't eat. If you eat constantly and feel out of control, you are obsessing about food because you tell yourself you shouldn't eat. Structuring your eating schedule by three meals and two snacks allows for more control and less obsessing. You may obsess about food, however, to avoid thinking about something unpleasant, such as your lack of assertiveness, fears, or pain.

SELF EVALUATION:

1. **If I were not obsessing about food or my weight, I would have to think about:**

    a. *My father's suicide.*
    b. *How much I hate my job.*
    c. *My problems.*

2. I obsess about:

    a. *What I can or cannot eat.*
    b. *Being perfect and not making a mistake.*
    c. *My weight.*
    d. *Everything.*

3. Beliefs that I have which contribute to my obsessive thinking:

    a. *What I eat defines my identity.*
    b. *It is awful to make a mistake.*
    c. *I need to lose weight in order to make myself feel better about myself.*

4. Thoughts that I could use to be less obsessive:

    a. *I am more than what I weigh.*
    b. *My only mistake is not allowing myself to make a mistake.*
    c. *I am worthwhile without having to lose weight to prove it.*
    d. *When I give myself permission to do what I want, I have less time to obsess about anything.*

5. Action I can take to change my obsessive thoughts:

    a. *When I obsess about something, stop that thinking and switch to a more pleasant thought.*
    b. *Allow myself to have pleasures so that I don't have to be so obsessed about what I am denying myself.*
    c. *Allow more variety in my life, so that I don't have so much time to think about my obsessive thinking.*

6. Things I fear if I give up my obsessive thoughts:

    a. *I will think about other things scarier to me.*
    b. *I will spend more money or take actions that are more destructive.*
    c. *I will not think about my weight, which will cause me to gain weight.*
    d. *I don't know what else to think about.*

EXERCISES:

1. Wear a rubber band around your wrist and when you start to obsess about something, pull back the rubber band, snap your wrist gently and say, "Stop that thinking." Switch from obsessive thoughts to nurturing thoughts.

2. Name the obsessive thoughts you now have. On scale of 1-10, how do you feel? Visualize yourself not having these thoughts. On a scale of 1-10, how do you feel not having the obsessive thoughts? Feeling better is a good reason to give up the obsessive thoughts.

3. Journal your thoughts or feelings about obsessive thoughts.

4. For additional help, read <u>Full Lives. Women Who Have Freed Themselves from Food and Weight Obsession</u> by Lindsey Hall, or <u>My Body/Myself: Body Image Guide for Teens</u> by Kathy Bowen Woodward.

Overcome Your Perfectionism

Perfectionism is a common problem for people with eating disorders. Common types of perfectionism include feeling stressed and driven by fear of failure, feeling you need to impress others in order for them to accept you, and feeling as if you can't make a mistake. People with perfectionist issues never feel satisfied. No matter how good you are, you never feel content. Even if you nearly reach your goal, you feel dissatisfied because it was not good enough. When you lost 30 pounds, you didn't feel proud or good about it because you needed to lose 35 pounds. This is all or nothing thinking without the grays.

Anorexics are at extremes with their perfectionism. They have to be the best, the slimmest, smartest, resulting in their being hard on themselves. Making a mistake is not acceptable; therefore, they avoid risks and become rigid in their thinking and actions. When they make one mistake, it is inexcusable and dramatic for them.

Perfection is different for bulimics and binge eaters because they don't need the order of anorexics. In fact, bulimics and binge eaters often say,

"You should look in my closet, you would see I am not a perfectionist." As you get to know them, however, you see their critical manners and fear of making mistakes. Their inability to accept their mistakes may lead them to binge or purge. It's important to allow yourself to not have to excel in everything. Using others' expertise to supplement your shortcomings is important too. It takes some of the pressure off you.

SELF EVALUATION:

1. Ways I try to be perfect:

a. Physical:	*Perfect face, figure, and dress.*
b. Achievement:	*Must achieve goals and not make mistakes.*
c. Perceptions:	*Impress people for them to like me.*
d. Emotions:	*Ashamed of negative feelings.*
e. Obsessive:	*Everything must be perfect around me.*
f. Self-esteem:	*Feel inferior to others.*
g. Relationships:	*Feel I should never argue or fight.*
h. Entitlement:	*Upset when others don't do what I want.*
i. Romance:	*Difficult to have a lasting relationship when I feel I am not good enough.*

2. Results of my trying to be perfect:

a. Mood swings.
b. Depression and anxiety.
c. Loneliness and difficulties forming intimate relationships.
d. Excessive frustration and anger.
e. Difficulty learning from my mistakes.
f. Rigid. Afraid of trying new things.
g. Never satisfied.
h. Lonely. Others don't like to be near me.

3. Beliefs that contribute to my perfectionism:

a. It is not O.K. to be second best.
b. It is not O.K. to make mistakes.
c. Need to impress others.
d. I compare myself to others and have to be the best.

4. Beliefs which I could have to help overcome my perfectionism:

    a. Where I place is not as important as always doing my best.
    b. It is OK to make mistakes. The only mistake is not to try.
    c. When I learn to accept myself as I am, the need to impress
       others will lessen.
    d. Giving up my perfection will allow me to feel better.

5. Fears I have of giving up my perfectionism:

    a. I will become fat.
       (I encourage you to challenge this thinking.)

    b. I will become lazy and not try hard.
       (Is it possible that you are trying too hard?)

    c. No one will like me.
       (People will like you better because most people do not
       enjoy being around people who are always trying to be
       perfect. They are not as much fun as others.)

6. Action I can take to overcome my perfectionism:

    a. Change my negative thinking
    b. Enjoy the present instead of looking always to do better.
    c. Look for answers from within rather than outside myself.
    d. Allow myself to make mistakes instead of beating myself up.
       (Your mistakes indicate you are taking some risks.)

EXERCISES:

1. Visualize yourself without pressures you now have to be perfect. Imagine yourself celebrating the fact that you made a mistake and learned from that mistake. On a scale of 1-10, how does this feel? How do you make this happen?

2. Make a list in your journal of ways you try to be perfect. After each, write what action you could take to be different. Use a colored pen to indicate when you are having to be perfect.

3. For additional help read <u>Your Perfect Right</u> by Alberti and Emmons or <u>Perfectionism: What's Bad About Being Too Good</u> by Miriam Adderholt Elliot or <u>Otherwise Perfect: People and their Problems with Weight</u> by Stuart and Orr.

Change "Shoulds" to "Choices"

We often lead our lives by what we think we should do rather than allowing ourselves to have choices in our decisions. When we don't give ourselves choices, we tend to rebel against our "shoulds." Whenever you say you should do something, ask yourself, who says you should? Is this your mother, father, boss, or church speaking? Once you make the decision to do something or not do it, you feel much more in charge of your life rather than feeling someone else is making decisions for you. This does not mean that you can always do whatever you want, especially when there are young children dependent upon you. However, when you change your thinking from "should" to having a choice, you feel much less resentful and less likely to turn to food.

Whenever you need to make changes in your eating or your weight, you often are ambivalent about these changes. There is a part of you that wants your weight to change, but another part that resists making the effort to change. It is important to recognize these ambivalent feelings and to give yourself choices.

Anorexics live by their "shoulds" without giving themselves choices. It is a way they feel they are in control of their lives. Bulimics and binge eaters also do not allow themselves choices without feeling guilt with regard to their food choices. Every morning, they say they should start a new diet or start exercising. They feel they have no choice and then they rebel against the "shoulds."

SELF EVALUATION:

1. When are the times I say I should do something?

    a. When I feel I need to lose weight.
    b. When I am not feeling secure within myself.
    c. When I try to please others.

2. **How do I feel when I should do something? How do I feel when I have a choice?**

   a. *I feel less resentful and freer when I have a choice.*
   b. *I feel more in charge of my life when I have a choice.*
   c. *When I say I should do something, I most often don't do it.*

3. **What are the ambivalent feelings I have about making changes about my weight and eating?**

   a. *I want to get out of my starvation routine, but I don't want to get fat. (Anorexic)*
   b. *I want to stop the purging, but I want to be able to eat all that I want without getting fat. (Bulimic)*
   c. *I want to lose weight and feel better, but I don't want to have to change my eating. (Binge eater)*

4. **What beliefs could I use to allow me more choices?**

   a. *My life can be productive even when I allow myself choices.*
   b. *I am the one in charge of my life not others.*
   c. *What is expected of me is what others believe, not necessarily what I believe.*

5. **Ways my eating is related to my living by "should" instead of choices:**

   a. *When I live by my "shoulds," it is often not what I want and then I turn to food to get what I want.*
   b. *When I say I should not eat, it sets me up for rebelling and overeating because I don't feel in charge.*
   c. *Every day I say I should eat this or I should not eat that, resulting in not feeling in control.*

EXERCISES:

1. Visualize yourself having choices instead of leading your life full of "shoulds" like you have been doing.

2. What situation can you be successful in making such changes? On a scale of 1-10, how does this feel to live your life by "shoulds?" By choices?

3. Make a list of your "shoulds." After each "should," write choices you can make.

4. For additional help, read <u>Real Gorgeous: The Truth about Body & Beauty</u> by Kaz Cook or <u>Good Girls Don't Eat Dessert</u> by Meadow and Weiss.

Change Your Attitude

Your attitude is the disposition you transmit to others. It is the way you see things mentally from within. The more you focus on positive factors in your life, the easier it is to remain positive and present yourself as confident and secure. If you focus on your weight as something negative, it influences how you carry yourself, present yourself to others, and consequently the response you get from them. A person not considered beautiful by physical standards can be regarded as beautiful with a cheerful and optimistic attitude. When you change your attitude toward your body and self, you will come across as more beautiful to others and to yourself.

Anorexics, bulimics, and binge eaters tend to get so preoccupied with their weight and food that it produces a negative attitude. I remember a client who had terminal cancer. She planned to make the most of what time she had, and she lived as though each day was her last. Her attitude helped to keep her alive much longer than was expected. So often we take for granted what we have and are not appreciative. When we change our attitude, we change our happiness and have more joy in our lives. I am very thankful for my parents modeling a positive attitude for me. My Aunt Madeline is also an inspiration for me. She is 83 years old and continues to be able to do many things because of her attitude. She enjoys life.

SELF EVALUATION:

1. **What are the attitudes my family presented to me? How do I repeat these same attitudes? Which have I changed?**

    a. *Don't trust people for they are out to get you.*
    b. *Enjoy life. You only live once.*
    c. *How one looks is the most important thing.*
    d. *Looking at a half-empty glass instead of a half-full glass.*
    e. *Seeing negative things and dwelling on them.*
    f. *Viewing life as dreary.*

2. **What are my positive attitudes?**

    a. *Love of life.*
    b. *Belief in people and myself.*
    c. *Enjoying the present.*

3. **What beliefs affect my attitude?**

    a. *Belief that I can't trust anyone.*
    b. *Belief that being pessimistic is realistic.*
    c. *Belief that having a negative attitude keeps me from being disappointed.*
    d. *Belief that I am not worthy.*

4. **What actions do I need to take to change my attitude?**

    a. *Change my thinking from negative to positive.*
    b. *Monitor my thinking to realize when I am negative.*
    c. *Observe others to see how their positive attitude helps them.*
    d. *Say I can instead of I can't.*

5. **What are my fears in changing my attitude?**

    a. *I will become phony.*
    b. *I will set myself up for disappointment. My negative attitude protects me from being disappointed.*
    c. *I have been negative for so long, it is comfortable for me.*

6. How is my attitude related to my eating behavior?

    a. My negative attitude makes me feel that I don't need
       to eat. (Anorexic)
    b. My negative attitude keeps me from enjoying life, therefore,
       I turn to food for enjoyment. (Bulimic)
    c. My negative attitude about my body says what difference
       does it make if I overeat. (Binge eater)

EXERCISES:

1. Visualize yourself having a positive attitude. How is this different from now? On a scale of 1-10, how does this feel?

2. Make a list of attitudes you have. Then make a list of attitudes you want to have. Next to the desired attitude, write what action you can take to obtain this attitude.

3. For additional help, read Courage to be Yourself: Growing Beyond Emotional Dependence by Sue Patton Thoele or How to Stubbornly Refuse to Make Self Miserable About Anything, Yes, Anything by Albert Ellis.

To Motivate Yourself, Take Action

If you have had failures with your eating or weight, it is difficult to make any changes. It is hard for the anorexic because she may need a medical emergency before she makes a change. Many times an anorexic seeks therapy only after passing out from not eating. Often, this is so scary she is willing for the first time to change.

Bulimics tell themselves each day they are not going to purge, just as the binge eater says that she will not binge. Doing what you have always done is comfortable. Thus, when you think of changes, make sure you start with changes where you know you'll be successful, not ones in which you'll fail. It is also important to take changes one comfortable step at a time. You don't get from one place to another by taking huge steps. When you think in terms of small steps, it is easier to get started. Giant steps make you feel overwhelmed.

Many people find it helpful to take ACTION instead of trying to motivate themselves. We often have more resistance to motivating ourselves than we do to the idea of taking action. The next time you tell yourself you don't feel motivated, change your thinking to what action you can take.

SELF EVALUATION:

1. **In what areas of my life do I need to feel motivated (or need to take action)?**

    a. *My eating habits.*
    b. *My negative thoughts.*
    c. *Lack of exercise.*
    d. *Learn new hobbies.*

2. **What little steps can I make that will be successful for me?**

    a. *Eat one more fruit for the week. (Anorexic)*
    b. *Eat one less treat for the week. (Bulimic and binge eater)*
    c. *Start exercising slowly, doing the kind of exercise I would most enjoy. (Binge eater)*
    d. *Start with a hobby I most enjoy.*

3. **What fears does this bring up for you?**

    a. *Change will be too slow.*
    b. *I am afraid I will do it for a while, then I will fail again.*
    c. *I am afraid I will succeed and then I will be expected to always succeed.*

EXERCISES:

1. Visualize yourself as motivated. What is the first step you can take to be successful?

2. Write in your journal feelings and thoughts regarding your lack of motivation.

3. For additional help, read <u>Anorexia Nervosa: The Wish to Change</u> by Crisp, Joughin, Halek, & Bowyer or <u>Weight Loss Through Persistence</u> by Daniel Kirschenbaum.

How Creative Thinking Can Improve Your Self-esteem

Creativity is the ability to trust yourself with a new way of thinking or creating, rather than imitating. When you feel empowered enough to believe in yourself, you are free to create and feel alive. The healthier you are, the more spontaneous and creative you are. The more you think about food and your weight, the less time you have for creative thoughts. An anorexic has a difficult time being creative because she needs to do things in the same way to feel as if she is in control. Bulimic and binge eaters aren't as creative as they would be if they were not preoccupied with their weight.

SELF-EVALUATION:

1. Ways I am creative:
2. Ways I would like to be more creative:

> a. *I'd like to take some risks of doing new things without fearing that I will make a mistake.*
> (<u>The fear of making a mistake is often worse than making one.</u>)

> b. *I'd like to be creative in the job and try some new things that I have not tried.*
> (<u>Go for it. You have only you to stop you.</u>)

> c. *I'd like to find new ways of eating, since the way I eat now isn't working for me.*
> (<u>A great goal for you. Good luck.</u>)

3. **Beliefs that keep me from being creative:**

   a. *I am not smart enough to think of new ways to do things.*
   b. *My ideas would not be good enough.*
   c. *Creativity is beyond my realm of thinking.*
      (Start with what you know most. This is the easiest way
      to start.)

4. **Beliefs that could help me become a more creative thinker:**

   a. *How do I know my ideas are not good enough if I don't give
      myself the right to think in creative ways?*
   b. *When I tell myself I am not smart enough to be creative, I
      am blocking my creative energy.*
   c. *Give myself permission to think new and creative ways
      rather than copying what others have said or done.*

5. **If I could become more creative, I would feel:**

   a. *More alive.*
   b. *Better about myself.*
   c. *Proud of myself that I could be creative.*

6. **Actions I can take to become more creative:**

   a. *Tell myself I can do it.*
   b. *Stop the thinking that says I am not good enough.*
   c. *Give myself time to allow creative thinking to emerge.*

7. **Examples of creative names I could give myself:**

   a. *Woman of size.*
   b. *Fabulous Fat.*
   c. *Woman of Stature.*
   d. *Sizeable Woman.*
   e. *Big, beautiful woman.*
   f. *Woman of weight.*
   g. *Woman of caliber.*
   h. *Big body, big heart.*

8. Examples of creative thoughts I could have:

   a. *A waist is a terrible thing to mind.*
   b. *Being a model means wearing clothes and not eating. I'd rather eat and take off my clothes.*
   c. *Scales are for fish, not women.*
   d. *I'm built for comfort, not for speed.*
   e. *Everything is beautiful...in its own weigh.*
   f. *Don't weigh your self-esteem.*

EXERCISES:

1. Visualize yourself as more creative. What would be one thing you could do to start? Start with an activity you feel the most passionate about. Imagine yourself being a computer full of information. Ask your computer self to talk to you. Allow your thoughts to surface. Enjoy the process.

2. Who do you know that is very creative? Talk to that person about what her thoughts are that allow her to be creative. What would work for you?

3. Write creatively in your journal.

4. For additional help, read <u>Enlightened Eating. Understanding and Changing Your Relationship with Food</u> by Rebecca Ruggles Radcliff.

Use Visualization to Obtain Your Ideal Weight

Visualization is the process of imagining what you wish to have happen. Realize that you are the only person who keeps you from fulfilling your dreams and aspirations. None of us ever reaches our full potential, but certainly all of us can do more to reach this potential. To imagine what we wish is often the first step in fulfilling it.

Many people imagine themselves at their ideal body weight and size in order to become the way they desire to be. You may imagine yourself eating less, feeling thinner, losing weight, gaining weight, eating healthy,

73

having healthy relationships, achieving the job you want, climbing a high mountain, or winning the gold medal at the Olympics. To visualize, you must first choose what you want. Secondly, you need to affirm it, saying, "I can --------------." Then, picture it as if it were true. I would never have written this book, had I not first visualized doing it. Then I took action to see my dreams come true.

SELF EVALUATION:

1. Dreams I have which I could visualize to become true:

    a. I'm at my ideal weight.
    b. I stay at my ideal weight.
    c. My weight isn't an issue for me.

2. The area in my life that is the most difficult for me to visualize being any different:

    a. I love my body.
    b. I have food as my friend.
    c. I have my weight stay at my ideal weight.

3. What actions can I take to have my dreams come true?

    a. Tell myself several times a day, "I love my body."
    b. See food as fuel necessary to make my body work and run properly just as my car does.
    c. Give myself credit for working toward a healthy weight.

EXERCISES:

1. Visualize yourself going to a family reunion as you now are. Imagine how you look and how you see yourself. What are you wearing? Who is at the reunion? Where is it? Take your time visualizing through your sense of sight. Next imagine the sounds you hear. What are people saying to you? What is the music you hear? What is the background noise? Now imagine the sense of touch. What does the outfit you are wearing feel like? The sofa you are sitting in? Imagine

all the things you can touch in the room. Now imagine the sense of smell. What food is there? What perfumes do you smell? What is your overall feeling about yourself and this experience? Now imagine yourself going to this reunion at your ideal weight and how you want to look. What are you seeing, smelling, touching, and feeling differently? You can react differently and feel differently when you visualize the changes. What feelings did this visualization bring up for you?

2. The next time you are upset and feel out of control, visualize yourself in a place and time when you were most comfortable with yourself and loved yourself the most. Visualize through sight, sound, smell, touch, and the overall feelings of that time. Bring those feelings to the surface as if you were at that place and time now. It is a very helpful thing to do. My place of serenity that I like to go to is a place in the mountains by a stream filled with evergreen trees. Some people like to visualize their marriage, the birth of their child (not the labor), or their ideal weight. When is a time you can bring beautiful memories to achieve these same feelings?

3. For additional help, read Creative Visualization by Shakti Gawain.

Daily Affirmations to Love Your Body and Self

Start your day off with an affirmation or a positive statement. You are beginning your day with a greater chance of success. Some people prefer to use the same affirmation over and over until it is a belief system that becomes automatic. Other people prefer to use a different affirmation each day. The choice is yours. I encourage my clients to state their affirmation during the day as well. For example, each time they go through a doorway, they are encouraged to repeat the affirmation. It is O.K. to say it even if you do not believe it at first. When my clients first use, "I love my body," they most often don't believe it. After saying it often to themselves, however, they do begin to believe it. Choose an affirmation about your self, body, and weight. Say the affirmation each time you go through a doorway. You may choose one of the following or create one of your own.

Affirmations

1. I love my body.
2. I love myself.
3. I am a worthwhile and lovable person.
4. I have a pretty face.
5. I have lovely hair.
6. My eyes shine.
7. My smile is warm and comforting to others.
8. My breasts are attractive.
9. My hands and nails are attractive.
10. I have the right to say "no."
11. Life isn't motivated by fear.
12. I have the right to all my feelings.
13. There are no bad feelings.
14. I have the right to make mistakes.
15. There is no need to smile when I feel like crying.
16. I have the right to change and grow.
17. It is O.K. to be relaxed, playful, and frivolous.
18. I have the right to change and grow.
19. It is important for me to set limits and boundaries.
20. I can be angry with someone I love.
21. I can take care of myself, no matter where I am.
22. It is O.K. to love myself.
23. I do have the right to please myself.
24. I can live the way I wish rather than meeting others' expectations.
25. I enjoy being myself. I am sufficient.
26. I give others permission to disapprove of me without feeling malice toward them.
27. Excellence, mediocrity, and failure are not criteria for goodness.
28. I accept being human.
29. There is nobody in this world like me. I am unique and very special.
30. I have the right to terminate conversations with people who put me down or try to humiliate me.

EXERCISES:

1. The next time you criticize your body, think about what it would be like not to have that part of your body. Be thankful that it works for you. When you complain about your breasts being too large, look at the woman whose breasts were removed. When you feel that your arms are flabby, remember the vet who had his arms shot off and who no longer has arms. We often take our health and our bodies for granted until we are no longer healthy or we lose part of our body.

2. Take a situation you most want to change. Think of an affirmation related to that problem. Thinking you will do it allows for it to happen. Say the affirmation you choose each time you eat, brush your teeth, get in the car or any designated time.

3. Make a list of affirmations as you use them. You can then chart your progress.

4. For additional help, read Daily Affirmations for Compulsive Eaters: Beyond Feast or Famine by Susan Ward, Thin Book. 365 Daily Aids for Fat Free, Guilt Free, Binge Free by Jeanne Westin, or Beyond the Looking Glass. Daily Devotions for Overcoming Anorexia and Bulimia by staff and patients at Remuda Ranch.

Thought Patterns

TYPE OF THINKING	USUAL PATTERN (1-10)	ACTION TO TAKE (1-10)
Perfect Thinking	*Expect so much from myself that I often feel like a failure.* *(1)*	*Give myself permission to make mistakes.* *(9)*

TYPE OF THINKING	USUAL PATTERN (1-10)	ACTION TO TAKE (1-10)
Should vs. Choices	*I live by my "shoulds."* (2)	*Each time I say I should do something, give myself a choice.* (8)
Motivation	*I give up easily and hate to start anything new.* (2)	*Take action. Do not wait until I feel motivated.* (9)
Affirmations	*I say what I can't do.* (2)	*Say what I can do and then act on it.* (9)
Creative Thinking	*I copy others' ideas because I am afraid my ideas will not be good enough.* (3)	*Give myself credit for thinking of new ways to do things.* (9)
Visualization	*I rarely visualize what I want to happen.* (3)	*Visualize what I want to happen. Then do it.* (9)

C H A P T E R T H R E E

How to Express Your Feelings to Change Your Weight and Self-esteem

*T*he emotional aspect of you is as important as the physical aspect in determining who you are. The emotional self allows you to feel. Many people with eating problems have problems accepting their emotional side. I often hear women say they are too emotional. I ask them who tells them this and it is often the men in their life who are unemotional and in control of their emotions. Since the men are having difficulty with their emotions, they are unable to handle hers. Certainly, you want to have control of your emotions, but no so much that you are unable to express them.

Anorexics are starved for attention to get their emotional needs met. It is, however, difficult for them to receive the attention they so desperately want. They feel they don't deserve it. Anorexics are often cold, distant, and emotionless. They are so much in control of their emotions that they don't let anyone know what they are feeling. To feel is to hurt or to lose control. Somewhere the anorexic has learned it is better to control all emotions than to allow herself to become vulnerable and hurt. Many loved ones describe the anorexic's emotional development at a pre-adolescent level.

■■■

Bulimics often stuff their emotions by bingeing and purging. When you don't accept what you feel, you have to do something with your emotions. Many people indicate purging is like getting rid of feelings that are in the pit of their stomach. Before people can rid themselves of their eating problems, they often must first learn to accept their feelings, express them, and discontinue the practice of stuffing the feelings with food. Bulimics often purge their emotions to not feel any pain. Therefore, it is sometimes necessary for them to get emotional needs met before they give up the purging.

Binge eaters often feel that their out-of-control eating results from not being able to express how they feel. Assertiveness training can be helpful to you if you are an overeater. It is common for binge eaters to come from families where emotions were explosive. Binge eaters want their emotional needs met but often have a history of rejection, so they turn to food rather than to people.

Men often have eating disorders because they are unaware of what they feel or what to do with their feelings. When you ask many males with an eating disorder what they feel, they often respond with what they think. Men who eat too much say it is because they have no idea how to get their emotional needs met other than through food.

Satisfy Emotional Hunger in Ways Other Than Food

Emotional eating is when you eat to fulfill needs other than physical hunger. Emotional hunger is when the thought or smell of food sounds good even though your stomach is full. It is the emotional hunger of wanting to be loved, cared about, nurtured, needed, appreciated, and accepted for being who you are. When you eat food to try to get these needs met, you probably feel emptier because food did not fulfill what you needed. Think of your need to fill the emptiness inside you. What are ways you can fill these needs besides with food? For example, do you need to ask for a hug, kiss, someone to hold you, make love to you, or buy you flowers? If you need it, ask for it.

SELF EVALUATION:

1. **Ask myself before I eat, am I physically hungry or emotionally hungry? If I am physically hungry, eat. If I am emotionally hungry, ask, what am I hungry for?**

   a. *Attention.*
   b. *Love.*
   c. *Recognition.*

2. **Instead of eating to meet these emotional needs, I could:**

   a. *Ask for what I want from family or friends.*
   b. *Parent myself.*
   c. *Allow my feelings to be expressed instead of stuffed.*

3. **Healthy eaters are different from me:**

   a. *They eat more than I am able to eat. (Anorexic)*
   b. *They eat when they are physically hungry.*
   c. *They usually can say no to food when they aren't hungry.*

4. **Action I could take not to eat for emotional reasons:**

   a. *Listen to my physical being to let me know when I am physically hungry. Eat only then, not for emotional reasons.*
   b. *Write in my journal when I feel like eating for emotional reasons rather than physical reasons.*
   c. *Meet my emotional needs from means other than food.*

EXERCISES:

1. Make a chart indicating when you are eating for emotional reasons so that you can be aware of your eating patterns. Paste a list of alternatives to eating on the refrigerator so that when you go to the refrigerator, there are other ideas of what you can do. Each time that you eat for emotional reasons, use this as way to learn more about yourself. If you don't try to understand what is going on, it will be difficult to change your behavior.

2. Write in your journal other thoughts and feelings you have about your emotional hunger.

3. For additional help, read <u>When Food is Love</u> or <u>Why Weight: A Guide to Ending Compulsive Eating</u> by Geneen Roth.

Identify Feelings

Below are examples of different feelings for you to learn to identify. Read the examples and write feelings expressed after-wards. Check your response to those listed below. Now start to evaluate your feelings throughout the day so you can learn to identify your feelings and express them instead of stuffing them with food.

1. I wish I had a nice figure like Mary.
2. I'd like to sock him in the face for calling me fat.
3. When I was a child, I used to hide in my room when my father would come home drunk. I didn't want to be hit.
4. I like my support group a lot. I will really miss the members when we move.
5. I feel so bad that I forgot my father's birthday.
6. I wish tomorrow were over. I don't look forward to being weighed at the doctor's office.
7. I found out today that I am pregnant. I've wanted to be pregnant for so long.
8. I don't think I will ever be able to be my ideal weight.
9. I didn't feel very comfortable when the seat of my pants ripped.
10. I didn't expect to win the lottery ticket.
11. It is hard for me to get up in the morning because I am unable to do things I love to do. I wake up in the middle of the night and can't get back to sleep. I'm unable to eat or my eating is out of control. I cry a lot.

Feelings expressed:

1. Jealous, envious	5. Guilt	9. Shame
2. Anger, rage	6. Afraid, fear	10. Excitement
3. Fear, anxious	7. Excitement, joy	11. Depression
4. Sad, unhappy	8. Despair, discouraged	

EXERCISES:

1. If it is difficult for you to identify your feelings, it may be helpful to start journal writing and underline feelings after you write about them. This helps you express your feelings. Underlining these feelings helps you to be aware of what your feelings are.

2. Visualize yourself being aware of what you are feeling. On a scale of 1-10, how does it feel to be aware of what you feel?

3. For additional help, read the <u>Deadly Diet</u> by Terence Sandbek.

Express Your Feelings

Feelings are often difficult for you to express, especially when you family didn't allow you to show emotions as a child. When a person accepts and expresses feelings, there is no need to ignore them or pretend that they do not exist. It is impossible to be assertive when you don't know what you feel. You can't express your feelings if you don't know what they are. One problem is that people tend to judge feelings as either good or bad. It's important to ACCEPT ANY FEELING THAT YOU HAVE AND NOT TO JUDGE IT AS GOOD OR BAD. There is no such thing as a bad feeling. It is important to monitor what actions you take as result of the feelings, but accept and acknowledge the feeling.

SELF EVALUATION:

1. Underline the feelings you have trouble accepting. Circle those that you have trouble expressing.

Anger	Daring	Fear	Lonely
Anxiety	Dependent	Guilt	Love
Brave	Despair	Giving	Lonely
Caring	Depression	Hate	Optimistic
Contentment	Energetic	Happiness	Pain
Compassion	Envious	Hurt	Persecuted
Coward	Excitement	Jealousy	Sad
Dangerous	Faithful	Joy	Shame

2. Ways I express my feelings:

    a. *Stuff them by eating.*
    b. *Crying.*
    c. *Telling the person how I feel.*

3. Beliefs that I have in regard to my feelings:

    a. *If I express my feelings, I will allow people to get too close and they will hurt me. (Anorexic)*
    b. *If I show my emotions, I will lose control. (Anorexic)*
    c. *If I show my emotions, I will be a cry baby and too emotional.(Bulimic and binge eater)*

4. Beliefs that I could have that would allow me to express my feelings:

    a. *I can show my emotions without losing control. By expressing my emotions, I will not have to exercise so much control. (Anorexic)*
    b. *If I share my feelings, people will know what I am like and will feel closer to me, and I closer to them.*
    c. *I can show my emotions without being too emotional.*

5. Fears I have in accepting and expressing my feelings:

    a. *I am afraid I will overwhelm myself if I get in touch with my feelings.*
    (It may help you to get in touch with your feelings so you won't feel overwhelmed.)

    b. *I am afraid I will be like my father who was always angry and exploding.*
    (Once you learn to express your anger in a healthy way, you can deal with the angry feelings without being out of control.)

    c. *I'm afraid that others will laugh at me because I don't know how to express myself very well.*
    (Share with a person you most trust not to laugh at you.)

EXERCISES:

1. Imagine an unwelcome feeling and welcome it into your life. Write what you might say to this feeling, telling it why you have been scared of it. Now write your feelings as you accept this feeling. Imagine it as a healthy thing for you to accept this feeling. Repeat with other feelings until you get comfortable with feelings without having to judge them.

    a. *"Anger, I am scared of you. I am afraid that I will be like my father whose anger scared me as a child. I know it is not good for me to bury you inside me because I then eat to stuff you instead of letting you out. I would like to be comfortable with you, but I'm not sure how to do this. My friend says that she is able to have her anger give her positive energy. I would like that too, but I need to know that you will not overpower me if I express you."*

    b. *Anger responds with, "I would like for you to express me because it feels awful for me to be pushed aside, ignored and then have all that junk food dumped on top of me. I don't like it. I don't like how I make you uptight when you don't express me. I would like to have you use me to give you energy. Let's work together on this."*

2. Write in your journal your feelings about the day. What upset you the most? What made you happy?

3. For additional help, read <u>Beyond Food Game</u> by Jane Latimer.

Grieve Your Losses

When you have a loss, it is important to grieve that loss. If you don't grieve, you may not be able to move forward. Each time that you experience a loss, you will also experience losses from the past that were not properly grieved. It is common for clients to say that they feel that they are over-reacting to a recent loss. When that is said to me, I encourage them to talk about past losses they have had, which they may be experiencing with this recent loss.

85

Sometimes when people do the proper grieving, they feel so much better that they are able to make changes in their eating habits. Many of my clients find it necessary to go through a grieving process when they change their eating habits. It is a loss for them not to eat the excessive sugars that they once ate. In order to make changes in your eating habits, you may need to grieve the loss of the eating habit you now have. Men often don't know how to grieve, nor do they have the support that women have. This results in turning to food to make them feel better.

1. Steps in grieving losses:

    a. Denial:

> 1. *I do not have a weight problem. (Anorexic)*
> 2. *Purging does not hurt me. (Bulimic)*
> 3. *Eating all those sweets is not harmful to me.*
>   *(Binge eater)*

    b. Anger:

> 1. *Why do people keep telling me to eat? (Anorexic)*
> 2. *Why can't I lose weight with purging like I used to*
>   *do? (Bulimic)*
> 3. *Why can some people eat what they want and never*
>   *gain weight and I have to struggle all the time?*
>   *(Bulimic and binge eater)*

    c. Depression:

> 1. *I wish I would feel better. I am so tired of being in*
>   *control all the time. (Anorexic)*
> 2. *When I stop purging, I get depressed so I start*
>   *purging again. It's a vicious cycle. (Bulimic)*
> 3. *It makes me feel so sad and upset that I can't eat*
>   *what I want without getting fat. (Binge eater)*
>   *(*<u>It is sad when your metabolism is not like the thin</u>
>   <u>person who can eat anything and not gain weight.</u>
>   <u>Grieving this may be necessary to accept this</u>
>   <u>fact and help you move forward.</u>*)*

86

d. Willingness to negotiate:

1. *If I eat dinner tonight, my parents will get off my back about eating. (Anorexic)*
2. *If I stop purging, I can still eat sweets. (Bulimic)*
3. *If I stop overeating, I'll lose weight and be O.K. (Binge eater)*

e. Acceptance of loss:

1. *I do have an eating problem. I have to change my ways of eating.*
   (It is a loss when you have to change anything you enjoy doing.)

2. *To stop bingeing is a loss for me. It is my choice whether or not I give it up.*
   (Anything to do with your eating is your choice.)

3. *I guess I am going to have to stop bingeing in order to feel better.*
   (Try it to see if you feel better.)

2. Losses I have had in the past, which I never grieved:

a. *Death of my father.*
b. *My best friend moving to another state.*
c. *My divorce.*
d. *My dog who ran away.*
e. *When we had to file bankruptcy.*

3. Beliefs that could help me grieve my losses:

a. *I need to move on, but I also need to give myself time to grieve.*
b. *When I pretend it doesn't hurt, I can't sleep. The hurt worsens when I try to avoid it. Facing my loss will help me move forward more quickly.*
c. *Grown-ups need to cry just as children need to cry.*

4. My eating is related to my grieving process:

   a. *When I deny my losses, I magnify their importance by forcing myself to not think about it. This results in my need to starve myself. (Anorexic)*
   b. *When I don't allow myself to grieve, I purge. (Bulimic)*
   c. *When I allow myself to journal or cry about my losses, I feel less need to stuff the feeling. (Binge eater)*

EXERCISES:

1. Allot a certain amount of time each day to journal, cry, get angry or whatever you need to do to grieve your losses.

2. Visualize yourself grieving your losses. Imagine yourself no longer feeling the pain, hurt, or loss that you now feel. On a scale of 1-10, how does that feel? What action do you need to take for this to happen?

3. Write a letter to the person or thing you have lost. What do you need to say to this person, food, weight, or fat? Then pretend to be that person or thing you have lost. What do you need to hear from them?

4. For additional help, read <u>On Death & Dying</u> by Elizabeth Kubler Ross.

Anger as Positive Energy

Anger is an emotion that many people are uncomfortable with and try to avoid or deny. Many people have learned to stuff anger for so long that they don't know when they experience it. Some people were penalized when they were children for expressing anger. Fear is another reason we stuff our anger with food instead of expressing it. We fear anger because we think it means we are immature or illogical. Anger, like all feelings, needs to be accepted. When we try to deny the feeling or judge it, we get in conflict with ourselves by saying that we should not feel this way. Remember that all feelings are natural and normal.

It took me a long time to accept my angry feelings. I felt trapped because my body said I felt angry but my mind said anger was bad. The conflict this presented for me was agonizing. Once I realized that there is no such thing as a bad feeling, I felt relieved.

It is O.K. to feel so angry that you would like to hit someone. What is not acceptable is to go out and hit that person. It is important to distinguish the feeling from the behavior. When you deny your anger, you give it more power than if you accept it. By saying you aren't angry when you really are, you haven't let go of the anger and it churns inside and grows. This anger later comes out as sarcasm, blowing your top, or eating out of control. When you don't allow yourself to express your anger, you may turn it inward. This can cause you to feel depressed. Your anger can become healthy energy when it is directed in a constructive way. Some of my most productive changes have resulted from anger I channeled into energy to motivate myself to make wise and healthy choices.

Males often express anger in a more explosive manner than females. Anger propels us to be rigid and unyielding in interpersonal relationships. The result is poor impulse control. When anger prevails, we often become intolerant of opinions different from our own.

Constructive anger can:
a. Release tension.
b. Help me communicate when I am upset.
c. Resolve hidden conflict.
d. Give me new ideas.
e. Alert me to threats.
Unexpressed or destructive anger can:
a. Disrupt my life
b. Control my thoughts.
c. Ruin my relationships.
d. Cause pain, health problems, and other emotional problems.
g. Leave a negative impression.
h. Cause a binge.

Ways to handle my anger:
a. Accept I'm angry and admit it to myself.
b. Identify the source of anger.
c. Understand why I am angry. Is it realistic?
d. Think about what I am going to say before I say it.
e. Change my negative beliefs that cause me to be upset.
f. Let go of the past and clear the way for a positive future.
g. State my needs so I don't have to be angry because the other person doesn't know how I feel.
h. Are my needs of being popular, loved, creative, challenged, and respect being met?
i. Do not attack the other person. State an "I" message of how I feel rather than a "you" message.
j. Do not bring up old wounds.

SELF EVALUATION:

1. What are the ways I handle my anger? How do I need to change?

   a. *I express my anger by hitting my children and spouse.*
      (Get help so that you can discontinue this practice.)

   b. *I kick, throw, or slam objects.*
      (Try talking about what angers you instead of acting it out.)

   c. *I buy glasses at garage sales and throw the glasses at the
      wall. I like to hear the sound of glass breaking.*
      (A client felt the release was worth the cleaning up of
      the mess.)

2. How do I need to change?

   a. *Instead of hitting people, I could tell them how I feel or
      punch a punching bag.*
   b. *Instead of kicking, throwing, or slamming objects, I could
      write in my journal how I feel.*
   c. *Instead of throwing glasses, I could scream.*

3. Ways I may block my anger:

a. *Be the nice guy. Don't make waves. I want to be universally liked.*
b. *I become isolated by never expressing what I feel.*
c. *My ignorance of what I am feeling contributes to my need for control or mastery. If I show my anger I might lose control.*
   <u>(When you are able to recognize and express your feelings, your need for control will lessen.)</u>

4. Behaviors I have that create anger in my relationships:

a. *Need to be right.*
b. *Negative criticism.*
c. *Passing judgment.*
d. *Threats.*
e. *Need for control.*
f. *Insecurity.*

5. Ways I can express my anger:

a. *Tell the other person when I am angry by stating how I am feeling. Send an "I" message" instead of a "you" message.*
b. *Write in my journal.*
c. *Think about what caused the feeling. Determine if it is rational. If it is not, change my thinking.*

6. Ways my anger gets stuck in my body:

a. *Weak heart.*
b. *Unhealthy eating.*
c. *Loss desire to exercise.*
d. *Illness.*
e. *Tension headaches and tense muscles.*
f. *Inability to sleep.*
g. *Inability to relax.*
h. *Tight muscles.*
i. *Binge or purge.*

7. **Think of a situation in which I was very angry. What was the negative belief that triggered the anger? What might have been the actual cause of the anger?**

    a. I felt I was discriminated against at work because I am fat. I didn't get the recognition that my partner got.

    b. Perhaps I wasn't discriminated against because of my fat. Maybe my coming to work late influenced my not getting the recognition she did.

    c. Maybe my attitude toward my fat is a factor more than my fat is.

8. **Beliefs I could have about anger that would be helpful for me:**

    a. Feeling anger has nothing to do with good or bad. Everybody feels anger at times.

    b. I will not need to let my anger get out of control if I talk rationally about my anger when it first occurs.

    c. When I ignore my anger, it is left inside of me and comes out in inappropriate ways later.

9. **My eating is related to my anger:**

    a. When I stuff my anger, I feel like I am losing control. (Anorexic)

    b. When I stuff my anger, I purge. (Bulimic)

    c. When I stuff my anger, I overeat. (Bulimic and binge eater)

EXERCISES:

1. Visualize yourself letting go of your anger. On a scale of 1-10, how does that feel?

2. Next time you are angry, write in your journal about it. Then talk to the person you are angry with so you don't have to keep it inside.

3. What would you like to say to your anger? What does your anger want to say to you?

4. For additional help, read <u>Anger Workbook</u> by Dr. Weisenger or <u>Dance of Anger</u> by Harriet Lerner.

Sob the Sadness

When you don't allow yourself to feel sad, you may experience depression. It is natural for everyone to have times when they feel sadness and need to cry to release it. When you don't cry or feel sadness in whatever way feels appropriate for you, you may use inappropriate methods such as overeating to squelch it. This, however, does not allow the sadness to go away. Allow yourself to feel the sadness so you can move forward.

I can remember when I used to feel sad, but I was afraid to express it because I felt if I ever began crying, I couldn't stop. (What a silly thought.) I have never met anyone who didn't stop crying sometime, have you? It was scary for me to admit I felt sad. I thought I was supposed to always feel good and I was weak if I allowed myself to feel my sadness. Clients often get very upset with themselves when they cry in session. They, too, have the idea that this is a sign of weakness. It isn't weakness--it is human.

You can tell when anorexics are getting better when they allow themselves to cry. It is very difficult for them to share their sadness with others. They are afraid they'll lose control. It also goes against their perfectionist thinking. Some bulimics and binge eaters deny their sadness, others feel they can't stop crying and feeling sad. Males may have been ridiculed for crying, so they have a difficult time expressing their sadness to others.

SELF EVALUATION:

1. What is it that makes me feel sad?

    a. When I have no friends.
    b. When I don't do as well as I would like.
    c. When I am not appreciated.
    d. When I am criticized.
    e. When others laugh at me.
    f. When I am not the best or the thinnest.

2. I express my sadness by:

    a. Crying.
    b. Talking to a friend about my sadness.
    c. Write in my journal about my feelings of sadness.

3. My beliefs about sadness that would be helpful to me:

    a. Sadness is not a sign of weakness. It's a normal feeling.
    b. I can feel sad and let go of it. Then there is no need to control it. It's when I don't allow my sad feelings to be expressed that I need control to keep them away.
    c. There is a difference between depression and sadness. Feeling sadness may help prevent depression, not cause it.

4. My eating is related to my sadness by:

    a. When I feel sad, I exercise so I won't eat. (Anorexic)
    b. When I feel sad, I purge instead of allowing myself to feel the sadness. (Bulimic)
    c. When I feel sad, I binge instead of allowing myself to feel sad. (Binge eater)

EXERCISES:

1. Take the last time that you felt sadness. What caused the sadness? What did you do about it? What could you have done differently? If needed, what do you still need to do to let go of the sadness?

2. Visualize yourself letting go of the sadness that you have from the past. Imagine it to be like your long hair that you cut off. On a scale of 1-10, how does this feel to let go of the sadness?

3. Write in your journal thoughts or feelings you have about sadness. List what makes you sad. What action do you need to take to express the sadness or let it go?

4. For additional help, read <u>The Courage to Grieve</u> by Judy Tertlebaum.

Decrease the Depression

Depression is common with people who have eating problems. In fact, it is the depressive feeling that leads people to eat in order to feel better. Anorexics' habit of not eating has similar symptoms to depression. Bulimics indicate that purging often serves the purpose of temporary relief from depression, although it only increases the depression. Binge eaters often overeat because they are depressed. Some people experience depression when they deny their feelings, especially when they turn their anger inward or block their sadness.

Depression can be a chemical imbalance, which is often evident from generation to generation. Your chance of experiencing depression is greater if family members also get depressed. Although your parents might have been depressed, they may not have known it. It is possible that they didn't have treatment available to them in their lifetime. If you have a chemical imbalance, it helps to increase your level of activity or an anti-depressant drug may be helpful.

Your negative thinking strongly influences your level of depression. If you have a negative opinion of yourself, you may feel your responsibilities are overwhelming. This can also cause depression. Look for ways to change your thinking from negative to positive. A positive outlook may be all you need to treat your depression.

SELF EVALUATION:

1. My signs of depression:

> *a. I cry a lot.*
> *b. I'm unable to go back to sleep when I wake up in the middle of the night.*
> *c. I lack energy.*
> *d. I feel hopeless.*
> *e. I can't feel joy, sadness, or anger.*
> *f. It feels like a dark cloud over my head and in my thoughts.*
> *g. Everything feels negative to me.*
> *h. Nothing is fun anymore.*
> *i. I don't enjoy life.*
> *j. Everything I do takes so much effort.*
> *h. I never laugh anymore.*

2. Beliefs that I could use to lessen my depression:

    a. I am in charge of what I can do to improve my life.
    b. Because things have not worked for me in the past doesn't mean they won't work for me in the future.
    c. Look at positive things rather than negative aspects so I will feel better.
    d. Being depressed doesn't make me a bad person.
    e. I can exercise and eat healthy foods to help me feel better and have more energy.

3. My eating is related to my depression:

    a. The more depressed I am, the less I eat. (Anorexic)
    b. The more depressed I am, the more I purge. (Bulimics)
    c. The more depressed I am, the more I overeat. (Binge eater)

EXERCISES:

1. Find out what family members have been depressed.

2. Visualize yourself not being depressed, but doing things you enjoy and would like to do. Reward yourself by doing pleasurable activities after you complete a couple things you don't want to do, but need to get done.

3. Put an "M" in front of what you have mastered for the day and a "P" for pleasure received so that you become aware of your progress. It also helps you to make sure you balance your life with pleasures and achievements.

4. When you feel overwhelmed or negative, review your thoughts. Change the negative to positive thoughts.

5. Make a list to organize things you can do to feel better. Prioritize the list. Keep it within reasonable limits.

6. For additional help, read <u>Feeling Good</u> or <u>Feeling Good Handbook</u> by David Burns.

Lessen the Anxiety and Fear

A generalized rather than a specific fear of something causes anxiety. The person is usually unaware of what is causing the uneasiness. Anxiety attacks can be very scary. You may break out in a sweat, have heart palpitations, feel as if you are having a heart attack, and experience an overall feeling of confusion. If you have feelings of anxiety, it is important to evaluate your negative and irrational thoughts. When you feel anxious, ask yourself what you are thinking to cause these feelings. Try changing your thoughts to affirmations and positive thoughts. Relaxation techniques may also be helpful to you.

Anxiety results from a need of approval from others or from the fear that you're not good enough. Sometimes a repressed conflict can also provide anxious feelings. Exercise, deep breathing, and relaxation techniques are helpful when you are anxious. Many people tend to overeat when they are anxious. It's important to calm yourself down before you eat so you will eat slower. You want to find ways other than food to calm yourself.

Overcoming your fears and anxiety takes time, but by breaking them down into manageable parts, you can overcome them. Have a solution that gives you a sense of control. When you are aware of your fear, ask yourself what action you can take in order to minimize the effect of the fear.

Anorexics are anxious and afraid they will get fat like a relative or gain weight they have lost. Many anorexics once were overweight. Bulimics are afraid that someone will walk in on them when they are purging. This would be very embarrassing for them. Binge eaters are afraid that their fat will cause others to discriminate against them. They project their feelings onto others and think others think this way because they feel so awful about their weight. The reality is that most people are so worried about their own life that they give others' weight little importance. Unfortunately, there are some who are unkind to obese people.

Males tend to have different fears and anxieties than females. Males fear loss of their job, poverty, ill health, death and aging. Females fear rejection, loss of loved one, and getting older. Both sexes may have fear of abandonment if they experienced the loss of a parent at an early age.

1. I become anxious and afraid when:

    a. I am unsure of myself.
    b. I am in new situations.
    c. I am not perfect or the best.

2. My body shows me that I am anxious:

    a. My heart beats so fast that I feel like I am having a heart attack.
    b. I start sweating and feel light-headed.
    c. My head feels as if it is spinning.

3. Beliefs that would help me become less anxious or fearful:

    a. Accept myself as I am rather than compare myself to others.
    b. Give myself permission to make mistakes and say mistakes are opportunities to learn.
    c. Allow myself to do the best that I can and if that disappoints others, that is their problem, not mine.

4. Action I can take to overcome my fears and anxiety:

    a. Relax more.
    b. Change my thinking from negative to positive.
    c. Reduce my stress.

EXERCISES:

1. Observe or interview people as to how they handle their anxiety in ways different from you. What could you do that they do to lessen your fears and anxieties?

2. The next time you feel anxious, take a deep breath. Breathe in through your nose and out through your mouth. This will help you to relax and be less anxious. You can also tense each set of your muscles, one at a time. After tightening your muscles, relax them.

3. Verbalize your feelings of fear to another. (It helps to lessen the fear.) Visualize yourself reacting to the fearful situation in the manner that you would like. On a scale of 1-10, how does it feel to let go of this fear? Now choose another fear and repeat the above exercises with another fear.

4. Write in your journal thoughts or feelings you have about your fears and anxiety. List things you fear or cause you to become anxious. After each item, indicate what action you can take to lessen the feeling.

5. For additional help, read Anxiety and Phobia Workbook by Edmund Bourne, Feel the Fear and Do It Anyway by Susan Jeffers or Love is Letting Go of Fear by Gerald Janpolsky.

Stop the Guilt

When my clients indicate that they experience a lot of guilt, I encourage them to think in terms of whose standards they are using to judge their behavior--their own or someone else's. Usually they think they should react one way when they feel something different. They feel guilty because of the disapproval they expect from others. It is important to think for yourself and not allow others to have that much influence on your decisions. Guilt is also evident when people don't feel they have choices. When you allow yourself choices, you generally lessen the guilt. For example, if you are going to feel guilty about having a piece of pie after dinner, let yourself have a choice. You can have the pie and enjoy it, you can have the pie and feel guilty afterwards, or you can choose to not eat the pie. If you choose to eat it, you want to be able to give yourself permission to eat the pie without guilt. Try to give yourself a choice that allows you not to feel guilty or rebel against not having a choice.

Anorexics feel guilty whenever they put any food in their mouth because they think they will get fat. Bulimics feel a lot of guilt about the money they spend on food they throw up. They also feel guilty about their purging secret and their cheating to maintain their weight. Binge eaters' guilt lies in their out-of-control eating and almost everything else they partake.

Males tend to feel less guilty about their weight and eating than females. This is partially due to our society, which is more tolerant of overweight males than females. One example is the push for some football players to weigh over three hundred pounds in order to have more weight to block or tackle. This is at the expense of the health of the players.

SELF EVALUATION:

1. What are my main sources of guilt?

     a. My weight.
     b. Worry I cause my loved ones.
     c. When I have been dishonest.

2. Beliefs that would be helpful to let go of my guilt:

     a. If I would give myself permission to eat a little, I would not have to feel so guilty. It is my thinking that eating is bad that causes my problems of guilt. (Anorexic)
     b. I purge as a way for me to release tension. I need to find another way to relax. My purging doesn't make me a bad person.(Bulimic)
     c. I am working on my bingeing, so I don't have to beat myself up and feel guilty about it. (Binge eater)

3. Fears I have of letting go of my guilt:

     a. Afraid I will lose control and get fat. (Anorexic)
     b. Afraid I will purge even more. (Bulimic)
     c. If I did not feel guilty, I am afraid I would binge even more. (Binge eater)

4. Action I could take to let go of my guilt:

     a. Admit my forbidden wishes and fantasies.
     b. Stop projecting my guilt on others.
     c. Don't let my guilt allow me to be manipulated or manipulate others.

5. My guilt relates to what I eat:

    a. I feel guilty whenever I eat anything. (Anorexic)
    b. I feel guilty about the money I spend on food. (Bulimic)
    c. I feel guilty about my deception of how I maintain my
       weight. (Bulimic)
    d. I feel guilty about the amount of food I eat when I am not
       hungry. (Bulimic and binge eater)
    e. I feel guilty about overeating.(Binge eater)

EXERCISES:

1. Write about your guilt until it is gone. After writing in your journal, pretend you are someone else reading your journal. What would you say to this other person? Is that what you also need to say to yourself? You want to be as nice to yourself as you are to your friends.

2. Visualize yourself letting go of your guilt. Imagine the guilt leaving your body. Enjoy the light feeling that you experience by letting go of the heaviness of guilt. What action do you need to take to let go of the guilt? On a scale of 1-10, how does it feel to no longer have your guilt?

3. For additional help, read <u>When I Say No, I Feel Guilty</u> by Manuel Smith or <u>Good Bye to Guilt</u> by Hopkins and Thetford.

Overcome the Shame

Anorexics feel shame because they expect themselves to be perfect, and they fall short of this perfectionism. It is humanly impossible to be perfect all the time. Bulimics feel shameful that they are deceiving others by maintaining their weight by throwing up. They are also ashamed of the amount of money they waste on food they do not keep down. Many of my bulimic patients have described it as similar to burning money. Male bulimics, especially athletes, tend to experience less shame than females. They often ask what's the big deal about purging? This may be the result of their coaches' attitude.

SELF EVALUATION:

1. I feel shame about:

    a. *Lies I tell about the amount of food I say I eat. (Anorexic)*
    b. *Money I waste on food and then throw it up. (Bulimic)*
    c. *The way I look and the way I eat. (Binge eater)*

2. I was shamed as a child by:

    a. *My parents singing, "She's too fat, she's too fat, she's too fat for me."*
    b. *Parents embarrassed me when they made me wear old-fashioned clothes to school.*
    c. *Brothers teased me about my weight in front of their friends.*
    d. *I was the fattest person in our school.*
    e. *I was the last person to be chosen for a team.*

3. Beliefs that I could have to eliminate my shame:

    a. *I am not responsible for anyone's behavior except my own.*
    b. *It is O.K. for me to make mistakes. Mistakes are opportunities to learn.*
    c. *I am more than what I weigh.*

4. Fears that I have in letting go of my shame:

    a. *I would not know how to think of myself without shame since it has been part of me for so long.*
    b. *My behavior will get even more out of control.*
    c. *My bingeing will get worse.*

5. My eating is related to my shame:

    a. *I feel ashamed when I eat anything. (Anorexic)*
    b. *I feel so shameful about throwing up that I purge to try to make me feel better. (Bulimic)*
    c. *I feel shameful about being so fat and that my children are embarrassed. (Binge eater)*

EXERCISES:

1. Visualize the feeling of not having the shame you now have. Let go of the shame as though you are removing it like tearing a page out of a notebook and crumbling it and throwing it away. Change your thoughts from "I deserve to be shamed" to "I don't need to have shame as part of my life. I will feel better without it." On a scale of 1-10, how does this feel?

2. Write in your journal thoughts and feelings about your shame. List ways you feel shameful. Next to each cause, indicate what action you can take to let go of the shame.

3. For additional help, read Healing the Shame That Binds You by John Bradshaw.

Lessen the Jealousy

Jealousy is a sign of possessiveness and a lack of trust. Jealous feelings generally arise from the perception that you aren't good enough. People with eating problems or distorted body images feel that they are not pretty or thin enough. They fear they are going to lose their significant other. As soon as a person improves her self-esteem, she usually feels less threatened by others and jealousy lessens. When a person compares herself with beauty pageant winners, most are going to feel as if they come up short. If you insist on comparing yourself with others, do not compare yourself only with the prettier or thinner ones. What a relief it will be for you when you don't need to compare yourself with anyone. Remember that jealousy is a feeling. Accept the feeling, don't judge it as bad. It doesn't feel good to be jealous, but it is a natural feeling that everyone experiences at times.

Anorexics feel jealous and feel threatened by anyone who is thinner than they are. They are likely to be competitive. Bulimics and binge eaters are jealous of persons who can eat what they want without getting fat. They wish they had a different metabolism. Males tend to be more jealous than females. Most males indicate they fear they'll lose their partner. The jealousy causes them to control their partners.

SELF EVALUATION:

1. When do I feel jealous?

    a. When I am not the thinnest, prettiest, or smartest.
    b. When my lover looks at another girl.
    c. When I feel inadequate.
    d. When I don't feel comfortable in what I am wearing or how I look. I then think everyone else looks much better than I do.

2. Beliefs that contribute to my jealousy:

    a. If I am jealous, I will try harder to be better.
    b. I am not as good as other people.
    c. I can't trust others.

3. Beliefs that could help me not feel jealous:

    a. Stop comparing myself to others.
    b. Accept and love me for who I am.
    c. I don't have to have the agony of feeling jealous in order to motivate myself to do better.

4. Action I could take so I could lessen my jealousy:

    a. Improve my self-esteem so that I won't need to compare myself to others.
    b. Change my thinking that I am not as good as others to appreciate my uniqueness.
    c. Love me for being me. Accept others for who they are.

5. My eating is related to my jealousy:

    a. When I see someone thinner than I am, I go for longer periods when I don't eat. (Anorexic)
    b. When I feel like I am not as good as someone else, I purge. (Bulimic)
    c. When I feel like I am not as good as someone else, I overeat. (Bulimic and binge eater)

EXERCISES:

1. Visualize yourself accepting your jealousy and letting go of it. On a scale of 1-10, how does it feel to let go of your jealousy?

2. Write in your journal your feelings and thoughts about your jealousy. List those things or persons that make you jealous. What action can you take to lessen the jealousy?

3. For additional help, read Jealousy by Clanton, Gordon, and Smith.

Show Compassion to Yourself

Anorexics, bulimics, and binge eaters show a lot of compassion for others, but are unable to show that same compassion for themselves. Anorexics have little compassion for themselves because of their high standards. Bulimic and binge eaters are generally compassionate to others because they are sensitive to what others feel. When other people make mistakes, you probably tell them that it's O.K. because they are learning. When you make a mistake, however, do you give yourself that same compassion? Probably not, but you also deserve understanding and compassion. It is important to treat yourself the way you would like to be treated by others.

Many men find it difficult to show compassion to themselves or others because they are afraid it is not masculine. Some see it as allowing themselves to be too vulnerable. They fear they will get hurt.

SELF EVALUATION:

1. How do I treat myself differently than I do my best friend?

    a. I am less patient with myself.
    b. I am more critical of myself.
    c. I don't discount feelings of others like I do my own.
    d. I listen to others' feelings, but I don't acknowledge my own.
    e. I am compassionate to others, but not to myself.
    f. I don't get angry with others like I get angry at myself.

2. **How would I like my best friend to treat me?**

    a. Accept me as I am.
    b. Not put high expectations on me.
    c. Be supportive of me.

3. **What keeps me from treating myself this way?**

    a. I guess nothing. I never thought of treating myself as I treat my best friend.
    b. My weight.
    c. Feeling I don't deserve it.

4. **What beliefs do I need to change in order for me to be able to show compassion for myself?**

    a. Belief that I don't deserve compassion.
    b. Change my hate of myself to love energy.
    c. Belief that it is self-centered to show as much compassion to myself as I do to others.
    (This is self-loving, not self-centered.)

5. **My eating is related to my lack of compassion for myself:**

    a. I feel I have failed when I eat. (Anorexic)
    b. After I purge, I hate myself. (Bulimic)
    (That is when you most need compassion.)
    c. When I overeat, I don't deserve any compassion.
    (That is when you most need it.)

EXERCISES:

1. Observe a healthy person who shows compassion towards herself. What can you learn from her? What does she do or not do that would be helpful for you to do?

2. Evaluate the last time you were hard on yourself and didn't show any compassion. Now take the same situation and show compassion. What was the difference after showing yourself compassion?

3. Visualize yourself showing compassion toward yourself. Imagine treating yourself in the most comforting, compassionate way you can. On a scale of 1-10, how does this feel?

4. Journal other thoughts and feelings you have regarding compassion.

5. For additional help, read <u>Compassion and Self-Hate</u> by Theodore Issac Rubin.

Balance Contentment with Happiness

When a client tells me that she wants to achieve happiness as a goal in therapy, I ask her to reevaluate her goal. When I used to have happiness as my goal, I always came up short. Certainly, I was able to be happy much of the time, but I don't believe happiness is achievable all the time. Contentment is much easier to achieve and doesn't have the fluctuations that happiness does. You can be happy part of the day, but probably not the entire day. You can experience contentment throughout the day. Wishing to be happy is like trying to find the reward at the end of the rainbow. Looking forward to that happening may keep you from enjoying the process of getting there.

Anorexics often appear to be happy and content. They want others to think that they have their act together. But, they rarely experience contentment or happiness except when they have lost weight or haven't eaten. This is short-lived because their critical attitude soon reappears. Bulimics and binge eaters could be more content and happy if they could start loving their bodies and not be critical of their weight. It is hard to be content when you are always criticizing your weight. It is equally as difficult, if not more difficult for males, to find contentment. Circle the following, which provide happiness for you. Underline those that you would like to have, but don't have yet.

Adventure	Health	Relationships
Assertive	Integrity	Self-esteem
Challenge	Money	Sexuality
Friends	Nature	Spirituality
Fun	Optimism	Work
Growth	Personal Goals	

SELF EVALUATION:

1. **What areas of my life do I now feel content?**
2. **What areas of my life am I not content and need to make some changes?**

   a. *Change my weight or my attitude toward my weight.*
   b. *Change my eating so I am not out of control.*
   c. *My relationship with my spouse contributes to my overeating.*

3. **What beliefs contribute to my lack of happiness?**

   a. *Need to be happy all the time.*
   b. *Always wanting more. Never satisfied.*
   c. *Never feel I am good enough because I don't give myself any credit.*

4. **What beliefs could allow me to be more content?**

   a. *Have contentment rather than happiness as a goal.*
   b. *Be as patient with myself as I am with others.*
   c. *Believe that I deserve to be content.*

5. **Action I could take to feel content and happy:**

   a. *Change my negative thinking to be more positive.*
   b. *Enjoy what I have rather than always wanting it to be better.*
   c. *Accept me for who I am rather than always needing me to be better.*

6. **My eating is related to my lack of contentment and happiness by:**

   a. *I am never satisfied with myself so I starve myself.(Anorexic)*
   b. *Since I am not happy, I eat to make me happy, but it only makes me feel worse. (Bulimics and binge eaters)*
   c. *I feel eating is the only happiness I have. (Binge eater) (It certainly would be foolish to give up your only source of happiness. See if you can find other sources of happiness so that food is not the only important part of your life.)*

EXERCISES:

1. Visualize yourself content. On a scale of 1-10, how does this feel? What are you doing? Thinking? Feeling? How do you make this happen? Good luck in achieving the contentment you desire and deserve.

2. List your personal assets, blessings, and ways that you are happy. Next list what you want to add to your list. Then go for it!

3. Journal other thoughts and feelings in regard to being happy and content.

4. For additional help, read Happiness is An Inside Job by Ken Keyes.

Journal Writing

Journal writing can be a useful tool to help you learn to identify and express your feelings, solve problems, and gain insight. It allows for catharsis just as talking to a friend or therapist provides relief from stuffed feelings. Some like to use their journal only when they are stuck in an attempt to find a solution to a problem. It helps to clarify their thinking. Journal writing is a way to become introspective instead of depending on others. People who have disturbing dreams often find these dreams lessen after they start writing about what is bothering them. When a person ignores what's bugging them, it comes out in other ways such as anger, jealousy, nightmares, or bingeing.

Many people throw their journal away after writing for fear others might find it and criticize what they write. Others like to keep their notes and look back on them as a means for charting their progress or finding answers that worked for them in the past. What you write and how you write is your choice. You don't have to make complete sentences, capitalize, or punctuate. This is an opportunity for you to explore your creative thoughts. By doing the exercises in this book, you are learning to journal.

Some people like to start or end their day by writing in their journal. Also a journal is something that can be very private. Since you are the one who writes in it, you can always depend on you to be there. A friend, however, may not always be available for you. Many people find their journals to be their special friend. I recall a client who came to a group session and had misplaced her journal. She was very upset. She said it felt as if she had lost her best friend. Her journal had become a way to relieve her anxiety, get in touch with her feelings, and help her take necessary action. She had become her own best friend through her journal.

If you feel stuck and are unable to get started, write about that. An example of what you can write is: *I am not sure what I am feeling at this moment. In fact it feels as if I am not feeling anything. I don't know what's going on with me. I feel numbed. Oh, that's a feeling. I don't feel stuck anymore. I have been eating all day.* Then start describing your feelings regarding the important parts of your day. What were the things that bothered you most about the day? What happened before you binged? Try to be open-minded about your day, but write about how you felt about the event. What were the feelings that occurred?

SELF EVALUATION:

1. Reasons I give to not write in my journal:

  a. *I am not a good writer.*
  b. *I am afraid someone will read it.*
  c. *I do not have enough time.*
      (Some people find it helpful to journal prior to bingeing or purging. They find that journaling takes no more time than bingeing and purging.)

2. Ways I could overcome these obstacles:

  a. *I can have my journal writing as a priority, just as I do my eating. If I didn't think so much about eating, I would have more time to journal.*
  b. *I don't have to be a good writer in order to journal. There is no right or wrong way. It's whatever works for me.*
  c. *I could throw away my journal after I write it or hide it in a place such as a safe so no one can read it.*

110

3. Benefits that might occur to me if I do write instead of eating:

    a. When I express my feelings on paper, I no longer need to stuff the feelings with food.
    b. It delays my bingeing.
    c. I become more aware of what I feel and think.

EXERCISES:

1. Keep a journal of your food, feelings, or thoughts. Some people find writing a food journal for a couple of weeks is helpful to gain control of their eating. If you do write what you eat, it can be helpful to use different colored highlighters for the various food groups. Also be sure to include the feelings you have before and after eating.

2. Visualize yourself using your journal to write your inner thoughts. Imagine feeling much better, having a sense of relief after writing, and being your own best friend. On a scale of 1-10, how does this feel?

3. For additional help, read <u>Journal to the Self</u> or <u>The Way of the Journal: A Journal Therapy Workbook for Healing</u> by Kay Adams.

My Journal

Date: *October 1, 1997*

I had another bad day today. I had planned to start a diet and once again I failed. I ate so much today. I wanted to isolate myself from everyone. Overeating makes me feel lethargic and I don't care about anything. When is this cycle ever going to end? I feel helpless. I wonder if I am the only person struggling? I feel so alone.

Emotional Evaluation

FEELINGS	CAUSES (1-10)	ACTION TO TAKE (1-10)
Anger	*Comments about my weight.* *(1)*	*Tell people I don't appreciate the comments.* *(9)*
Anxiety	*Feeling that I'm not good enough.* *(1)*	*Tell myself, "I am sufficient."* *(8)*
Guilt	*Bingeing* *(2)*	*Tell myself I have choices.* *(8)*
Fear	*Weight gain and loss of loved one.* *(1)*	*Enjoy what I have instead of fearing its loss.* *(8)*
Jealousy	*Thinner people than me.* *(2)*	*Stop comparing myself to others.* *(8)*
Sadness	*Unable to cry about anything.* *(2)*	*Give myself permission to cry.* *(9)*

FEELINGS	CAUSES (1-10)	ACTION TO TAKE (1-10)
Hate	*I hate my body.* *(2)*	*Tell myself I love my body until I believe it.* *(7)*
Depression	*Feel so down about everything.* *(1)*	*Change my thinking.* *(8)*
Compassion	*Lack of compassion for myself.* *(2)*	*Treat myself like I treat my best friend.* *(9)*
Contentment	*Rarely do I have a sense of peace.* *(2)*	*Ask myself what I need and go for it.* *(9)*
Happiness	*My friends.* *(9)*	*Make sure to allow enough time with my friends.* *(9)*
Grief	*Loss of my parents.* *(1)*	*Allow myself time to grieve my loss.* *(7)*

CHAPTER   FOUR

Improve Your Relationships to Change Your Weight and Self-esteem

$\mathcal{S}$ociety has played a huge role in how people view their bodies. In the late 1800's it was stylish to be round and robust. The wealthy ate large volumes of food since they were the only ones able to afford to eat in such a manner. Marilyn Monroe was the example of the sexy idol of the 50's, with a round, full body. Twiggy was the thin model in the 70's who changed how society looked at thinness. This role model has made many young girls want to achieve the thin look, which is unnatural and unhealthy.

Our social self includes not only our family, but also our friends and the many people in our lives that have been an influence. It is important to understand your family, including your mother, father, and siblings, in order to understand whether they have played a part in your eating disorder. When we have relationship problems with others, we often bring those difficulties into our relationship with food.

■■■

The reason most people don't have problems with food when they are in love is that they get their emotional needs met by the other person. When people don't get these needs met in relationships, food takes its place. You may not be able to give up your relationship with food without first having a successful and healthy relationship with others. The more you meet your needs, the less you have to depend on food.

Some people have stronger social needs than others. Anorexics tend to isolate themselves. Their relationships with others are often involved around their feeding them. It is a sense of pride that they are able to have control and not eat as they prepare elaborate food for others. Anorexics often bring large amounts of food to the office for people to eat. It is difficult for them to get close and have healthy relationships because they fear others may hurt them.

Bulimics and binge eaters are generally more gregarious and outgoing than anorexics. They are people pleasers, try to fix things for other people, and frequently are the nurturing types. Helping the bulimic and binge eaters to treat themselves as they treat others is the challenge. They often are skilled in helping others without having a clue how to help themselves. They are so busy trying to fix things for others that they forget about meeting their own needs.

Men tend to be more influenced by large muscles than by thinness. When men don't have the large masculine build, they feel that they aren't as good and are more prone to an eating disorder or steroid use. Men with eating disorders tend to have experienced negative reactions to their bodies from their peers while growing up. Teasing by their peers is often the beginning of their eating disorder. Adolescent males develop anorexia or bulimia because they fear their peers will reject them if they are too fat or different from their friends.

How Your Family Affects
Your Weight and Self-esteem

Your family of origin has influenced who you are. Those behaviors, both negative and positive, that your family taught you will be easy to repeat. It takes a conscious effort to change those qualities that you didn't like about your family.

Your family influenced your thoughts about yourself, body, and eating habits. Your mother modeled such things as how she carried her body, what she ate, and statements she made about your looks and weight. Your father's response to your mother and her body also influences how you feel about your body. Comparing yourself to your siblings may also influence how you feel about yourself and your body.

Anorexics were once thought to come from achievement oriented upper-middle class Caucasian families. Recent evidence suggests that the disease is more widespread, affecting all sectors of society. Anorexics generally come from families who ignore their problems rather than work them out. This causes the anorexic to think that she has come from this "perfect" family. However, it becomes clear that no resolution ever occurred within the family because they denied that any problems existed. When a family sweeps problems under the carpet and tells themselves they are the perfect family, each member wonders what's wrong with me because I don't feel O.K.

Anorexics often have mothers who are very involved and controlling in their daughter's life. The anorexic learns that her eating is one area in her life that her mother can't control. Enmeshed with her mother and distant with her father is often the case. Much of the time she wants to get close to her father, but he doesn't allow it and he may be distant. This causes the anorexic to become distant with others. She tries to get her father's approval. Some anorexics starve themselves to be like the son they felt their father wanted. Most anorexics feel they have always been the perfect daughters--getting A's in school, causing parents no problem, and always being agreeable. Anorexics are often only children. If there are siblings, the female anorexic tends to be very competitive with siblings, especially her sisters.

Bulimics' and binge eaters' families are often very chaotic and their lives are out of control. The families often tend to be large, not giving the children the attention they want and deserve. The families are so chaotic that the bulimic learns to be comfortable with chaos. Bulimics' and binge eaters' mothers are generally not overly involved in their daughters' lives. They often are closer to their fathers than their mothers. Bulimics and binge eaters often come from alcoholic or depressed families. The chemical imbalance, which contributes to depression, can also contribute to the eating disorder.

The families of males with eating disorders parallel the female's family in that the anorexic male's family may be rigid and controlling. The male bulimic and binge eater's families tend to be chaotic and out of control. They are unaware of what is a normal family.

117

Healthy Family Characteristics

1. There is closeness in the family.
2. Family members allow each family member to be unique.
3. Family members accept others' feelings when different from their own.
4. Each person in the family feels loved and accepted.
5. Family is good at resolving problems.
6. Family is happy most of the time.
7. Family laughs, plays and has fun together.
8. Family members are supportive and encourage one another rather than making fun of each other.

SELF EVALUATION:

1. My family differs from the healthy family:

    a. We have to be what our parents want us to be.
    b. Parents argue all the time.
    c. Siblings fight constantly.
    d. Father is distant and mother is over-involved in my life.

2. What I learned from my family regarding who I am:

    a. I am a useless, worthless, and will never amount to anything.
    b. I am to be seen but not heard.
    c. I am too fat.
    d. I am never good enough.

3. Eating habits and attitudes toward my body that I learned from my family, which I wish to continue:

    a. Meal times are times to eat together and enjoy one another.
    b. Social times can include enjoyment of eating together.
    c. Physical appearance is important because it is the first impression you make, so have your first impression be positive.

4. **Eating habits and attitudes toward my body which I learned from my family which I wish to discontinue:**

   a. *Eating fast.*
   b. *All social events have to revolve around an abundance of food.*
   c. *Do anything not to be fat.*
   d. *Eat because you are too skinny.*
   e. *My mother was critical of her body and mine.*

5. **What messages did my mother give me about her own body? My body?**

   a. *I hate my body. I am so fat.*
   b. *Be careful what you eat. You don't want to look like me.*
   c. *She spent hours fixing herself up to go to the grocery store.*

6. **What messages did my father give me about my body? Myself?**

   a. *He always complimented me about my appearance.*
   b. *He expected me to act and look like my brothers.*
   c. *He always negatively compared my body to my sister's body.*

7. **What messages did my siblings give me about my body? Myself?**

   a. *Sister would brag about how she was ten pounds lighter than I was. It never entered my mind that she was five inches shorter.*
   b. *Brothers would tease me about being fat and stupid.*
   c. *Sisters made me feel I was not good enough.*

8. **My eating and weight is related to my family:**

   a. *It is my way of rebelling against their control. (Anorexic)*
   b. *My metabolism is similar to my family's.*
   c. *Food is a source of reward in my family.*
   d. *I turn to food to feel better just like my family.*
   e. *I am overweight like my family members.*
   f. *My family laughs at me because I am overweight.*

119

1. Visualize yourself saying what you need to say to your family to let them know how you feel. Practice saying what you are going to say until you feel comfortable. On a scale of 1-10, how does it feel to say this? Say what you need to say for your sake and don't expect a certain response. This is for you more than for them.

2. Write in your journal your feelings about your family. Write a letter to any family member you have something to say. You don't need to send the letter unless you think it will be helpful. Sometimes the writing is enough.

3. For additional help, read <u>Father Hunger: Fathers Daughters and Food</u> by Margo Maine. or <u>Like Mother, Like Daughter</u> by Debra Waterhouse.

Life Line-Family History

In order to understand your eating and body image, it may be helpful to take a history of your family. Knowing what has happened in the past may give some understanding of your present situation.

SELF EVALUATION:

1. What other family members have similar problems with their weight as you do?

> *a. My sister is anorexic.*
> *b. My whole family is overweight.*
> *c. My grandparents and their parents were overweight.*

2. When did you first become concerned about your weight?

> *a. When my gymnastics coach told me I needed to lose weight.*
> *b. I always have been concerned about my weight, since my mother was always concerned about her weight.*

3. **Name the significant points in your life when changes in your weight occurred:**

   a. Gained weight:

   1. After each diet.
   2. After birth of each baby.
   3. When my father died.
   4. At college.
   5. When we moved.
   6. After break up with my boy friend.

   b. Lost weight:

   1. When I was in high school and in love with my first boy friend.
   2. When I had a job I liked.
   3. When I exercised and watched what I ate.
   4. After my divorce.
   5. When I went to Overeaters Anonymous meetings, Slim for Life Classes, Weight Watchers, or other weight reduction programs.

4. **Name the significant points in your parents and siblings' lives In which they had weight change:**

   a. Father gained weight after his father died.
   b. Mother gained weight after birth of each of her children.
   c. My siblings have always been heavy.

EXERCISES:

1. Make your lifeline using the table that follows.

2. Journal other thoughts or feelings about your family history:

3. For additional help, read Your Dieting Daughter: Is She Dying for Attention by Carolyn Costin or Preventing Childhood Eating Problems by Hirschmann and Zaphiropoulous.

My Life Line

AGE	SELF	MOM	DAD	GRAND MOTHER	GRAND FATHER
0-5	10# birth	9# birth	11 birth	8# birth	9# birth
6-12	5# +	10# +	20# +	15# +	10# +
13-20	2# +	20# +	30# +	15# +	30# +
21-30	5# +	45# +	10# +	15# +	30# +
31-40	10# +	60# +	20# +	40# +	35# +
41-50	40# +	45# #	30# +	30# +	35# +
51-60	60 # +	50# +	20# +	30# +	40# +
61-70	40# +	55# +	10# +	50# +	Died of heart attack
71-80		Died of cancer	10# (-)	Died of cancer	
81-90			Died of heart attack		

+ = over weight   (-) = under weight

How Families and Friends of a Person with an Eating Disorder Can Help

1. Be supportive, honest, and keep promises.
2. Do not push an eating disorder person to eat.
3. Compliment her strengths instead of her eating disorder.
4. Remember she wants control over her eating. Let her have control unless it is dangerous to her.
5. Talk in terms of alternatives and choices.
6. Remember that stress increases her need for food.
7. Have information concerning eating disorders available.
8. Remember that solutions are not quick. Be patient.
9. Do not allow family life to revolve around the eating disorder. Do not neglect spouse or other family members.
10. Don't become a martyr. Make sure you take care of yourself. Love the child within as you would like to be loved.
11. Admit your feelings. Send "I" messages about how your feel.
12. Join in family therapy.
13. Express honest love and affection to your child/spouse/friend.
14. Make sure you don't limit your discussions to her eating disorder. Don't punish or reward the illness.
15. Do not use manipulative statements. Do not put the person with an eating disorder down or compare her to others.
16. Realize that your loved one is probably ambivalent about getting help or changing.
17. Be gentle with yourself. Get help for yourself if you need it.
18. Do everything to encourage her initiative, independence and autonomy. Trust your spouse, friend, or child to find her own values, ideals, and standards.
19. Learn relaxation techniques to help you during stressful times.
20. Avoid arguments about food and weight.

For additional help, read Surviving Eating Disorder-Strategies for Family and Friends by Siegel, Brisman, and Weinshel, or Bulimia. A Guide for Friends and Family by Sherman and Thompson.

How to Let Go of the Past
in Order to Let Go of the Weight

Behind your fat is probably a great deal of hidden pain. For many, it is the pain of not getting your needs met during your childhood. For others, it is the result of abuse--sexual, physical, or emotional. Others find that their pain is the result of not having acceptance for who they are. (For example, the daughter whose parents wished for a son; the musician whose parents wanted an athlete.) Sometimes anger or rebellion is the result of the pain. The child who says to her parents, "If I embarrass you at 150 pounds, wait until I get to 300 pounds and see how you feel." The sad part of all this is that you are actually hurting yourself more than your parents. When your feelings are hurt, it is helpful to get in touch with the anger that someone has hurt you. When you are able to express this anger outwardly, generally you will not have to hurt inside.

Anorexics will deny they are in pain for fear others might try to make them change their behavior. Bulimics and binge eaters often use food as a means to comfort themselves from their pain. Instead of facing their pain straight on, they stuff it with food. Both bulimics and binge eaters tend to be very sensitive to others and have their feelings hurt easily. This causes more pain. Most males with eating disorders are more sensitive than the general male population.

It is important to realize that you can let go of past pain and hurt. You don't have to burden yourself with the heartaches of the past. When you feel victimized by the past, you avoid living in the present. As you let go of the past, you will trust yourself more, and feel more confident and self-assured. Frequently, as you let past anger go, you also let go of unwanted weight. For many, this is a necessary step before you can rid yourself of undesired fat.

SELF EVALUATION:

1. **What are some of the pains from the past that I need to let go?**

   a. My divorce.
   b. Sexual abuse.
   c. Ways my parents treated me.
   d. Ways my siblings ridiculed me.

2. What are the benefits of continuing to have these pains?

a. *Justifies my anger.*
b. *Can continue to have people feel sorry for me.*
c. *I guess there is no benefit to continue to have them.*
d. *It makes my parents feel guilty.*
   *(*It is hurting you more than your parents to continue to hold onto this pain.*)*

3. What are the benefits to give up problems of past?

a. *Feel freer.*
b. *Can enjoy living in the present rather than in the past.*
c. *Future feels brighter.*

4. How is my eating or weight related to these past issues?

a. *I get back at my parents by not eating. (Anorexic)*
b. *When I purge, it feels like I am ridding myself of these awful feelings from the past. (Bulimic)*
c. *Overeating is a way to protect myself from getting hurt again. (Binge eater)*

5. What beliefs can I have?

a. *Even though the past hurts and has been part of me for a long time, it doesn't mean I have to continue to let it be important to me.*
b. *I can change my thinking. Because it was important in the past does not mean it has to be important now or in the future.*
c. *I have the power to change my actions, beliefs, and thoughts today no matter what happened in the past.*

6. What action can I take to overcome these feelings?

a. *Write about them.*
b. *Talk to a friend or a therapist about it.*
c. *Grieve about my past so I can let go of it.*

EXERCISES:

1. Visualize yourself letting go of your past. Do one issue at a time. When you feel you are O.K. about one issue, then work on another. On a scale of 1-10, how does this feel to be able to free you of your past issues?

2. Journal your thoughts and feelings about letting go of the past.

3. For additional help, read Cutting Loose by Howard Halpern, Unfinished Business by Maggie Scarf, Losing Your Pounds of Pain by Doreen Virtue, or Eating Disorder Sourcebook by Carolyn Costin.

How to Develop Healthy Relationships

A healthy relationship is one in which you are encouraged and accepted for being you. Unhealthy relationships or lack of relationships may influence your need to overeat to fulfill your emotional needs. You choose relationships, which reflects how you feel about yourself. The more positive you feel about yourself, the more likely you will choose someone who will be a positive influence on you. If you don't like yourself, you are going to wonder why anyone should choose you. Then you will choose a relationship that proves you are unworthy.

Relationships can include relationships with persons of the same sex, the opposite sex, nature, family, friends, and acquaintances. Pets are tremendously helpful for many people with eating disorders because they accept you unconditionally and do not care about your weight.

Letting go of an unhealthy relationship may be necessary in order for you to move on with the rest of your life, including your eating. It may be too difficult to change your relationship with food until you change or get out of the unhealthy personal relationship.

Anorexics generally shy away from relationships because many have experienced unhealthy ones in the past. Some bulimics are promiscuous without getting emotionally involved in the relationships. Binge eaters tend to choose partners they can nurture and take care of rather than to care for themselves.

People with eating disorders often find that their relationships are not fulfilling their intimacy needs. Intimacy is the closeness shared with another person who allows you to be yourself and unconditionally loves you. Each partner who responds in ways different from what she feels, in order to please her partner, defines many relationships. This is an unhealthy expression, which prevents intimacy from taking place. Frequently, food is a substitute for this need. As a constant, food can make a person only feel temporarily better.

When you turn to food for intimacy, you may be shutting out people who can fulfill this need. An example of this is a bulimic patient who was engaged to a young man who insisted she get treatment for her disorder, or he was breaking the engagement. She was turning to food instead of to him. Once she was able to be intimately comfortable with him, she gave up her bulimic behavior.

Some people feel vulnerable when they let their guard down and fear they can easily be hurt. When you are intimate, you reveal your vulnerability. It is important to know when to allow yourself to be vulnerable (and be close) and when to raise your guard (so as not to be hurt). People who lack trust and who have been hurt often will not show their vulnerability.

Anorexics and binge eaters feel especially vulnerable because others comment about their weight. Many people use their fat to protect themselves from becoming vulnerable in a relationship where they might get hurt again. Others don't reveal their feelings so their vulnerability doesn't show. They feel safe, but are lonely and less trusting of themselves and others. Many people with eating disorders don't have healthy ways to assert or protect themselves from others. They don't know when or where to allow their vulnerability to show, so they never let others see it.

Your expectations of yourself and others often cause you to feel that you have failed. When you expect something from others but don't tell them, you are setting yourself up for a disappointment. Thus, you overeat to make yourself feel better. It is important that you don't expect others to live up to your expectations. They have their own expectations. If your partner says that no matter what he does it's never enough, you may be expecting him to fulfill your needs.

SELF EVALUATION:

1. **How is my lack of a relationship or a poor one causing me to get my emotional needs met through food?**

    a. *I eat to avoid relationships.*
    b. *I am in an unhealthy relationship in which I don't get my needs met, so I turn to food to feel better.*
    c. *Food is the only relationship I have.*

2. **What keeps me in this relationship or prevents me from getting into a healthy relationship?**

    a. *I don't think I deserve anything better.*
    b. *If I were in a healthier relationship, my partner might not allow me to boss him around like this partner allows.*
    c. *I have never been in a healthy relationship. I don't know how to be in a good relationship.*
    d. *Fear of being alone or fear I will not find anyone better.*
       (This is an unhealthy reason to stay in a relationship.)

3. **Has food had the same importance to me when I have been in a love relationship? What was different from what I experience now?**

    a. *We were doing a lot of fun things.*
    b. *It felt good not to have to turn to food to make me feel better.*
    c. *I received lots of affection and attention.*
    d. *I felt important.*
       (How can you feel important without being in a relationship?)

4. **What beliefs would help me with relationships?**

    a. *Just because relationships in the past have meant pain, hurt and rejection doesn't mean that all relationships have to be that way, if I do a better job of selecting a partner.*
    b. *If I change my thinking that I deserve someone kind, loving, and caring then maybe I will find someone like that.*
    c. *Relationships are not built on what my size is.*

128

5. **How have I sabotaged relationships in the past?**

   a. *Acting like I didn't care so that my partner would reject me.*
   b. *Haven't been available emotionally.*
   c. *Lying to my partner that I was busy so I could binge or purge.*

6. **My expectation of myself and others influences my eating and my weight:**

   a. *I starve myself when I don't meet my own expectations. (Anorexic)*
   b. *I purge when I don't get the praise I expect from others. (Bulimic)*
   c. *I overeat when I don't meet others' expectations. (Binge eater)*

EXERCISES:

1. Visualize yourself in a healthy intimate relationship. On a scale of 1-10, how does that feel? What do you need to do to have this happen? Make a plan and follow through with it.

2. Journal your thoughts and feelings about present and past relationships. Write what you have learned from past relationships to help you not make the same mistakes again.

3. For additional help, read <u>Too Good for Her Own Good: Searching for Self and Intimacy in Important Relationships</u> by Bepko and Krestan, <u>The Girl Within</u> by Emily Hancock, or <u>Dance of Intimacy</u> by Harriet Goldhor Lerner.

How Abusive Relationships Affect Your Weight and Self-esteem

When a person has experienced physical, sexual, or verbal abuse, they have also experienced emotional abuse. They wonder when the abuse will happen again and what they're doing to cause people to react in an abusive manner.

Abusers are angry people who have poor impulse control and are intolerant of opinions and beliefs that differ from theirs. Control issues are often a part of the problem and often lead to physical abuse. Some abusers feel they are entitled to control their spouses. Eventually, spouses begin to believe this too. Both the abuser and abused become confused as to how a family ought to operate since both have probably come from dysfunctional families where abuse was prevalent.

Shame follows abuse, whether you abuse or allow yourself to be abused. Frequently, non-nurturing parents have children who grow up feeling responsible for the family's dysfunction. She believes if she had been good enough, everything would have been all right. It is common for abusers or abused to come from families where there are abandonment issues. She would rather take the abuse than have the abuser leave her as a parent had when she was a child.

Abusers blame the abused for causing the abuse. They say, "It's your fault I hit you. I worked hard all day and when you didn't have the children quiet when I got home, you deserved to be hit." The abused starts believing this, loses her self-confidence, and makes it difficult for her to leave the abusive relationship. It is a manipulative relationship. The following are signs of an abuser, of which you might be a victim.

Signs of an abuser:
1. Jealousy: A sign of possessiveness and lack of trust.
2. Controlling behavior: Say it is because of concern for partner's safety, but is so the abuser can be in charge.
3. Quick involvement: Often wants to get married right away.
4. Unrealistic expectations: Expects partner to meet all their needs.
5. Isolation: Abuser tries to cut the abused off from all resources.
6. Hypersensitive: Claims feelings are hurt easily.
7. Blames others for problems: Tells the abused they are the cause of all conflicts.
8. Blames others for feelings: Abuser makes the decision about what the abused feels. Blames abused for the way abuser feels.
9. Cruel to animals and children: Insensitive to their pain.
10. Use of force in sex while the partner sleeps or is ill.
11. Verbal abuse: Demeans partner's achievements.

12.	Rigid sex roles: Abusers expect partners to serve them.
13.	Dr. Jekyll and Mr. Hyde: Sudden changes in mood.
14.	Past battering: Says hit in the past, but the abused made the abuser do it.
15.	Probably was battered as a child.
16.	Threats of violence: Excuse threats by saying everybody talks like that.
17.	Breaking or striking objects: Terrorizes the partner into submission.
18.	Any force during an argument: Any pushing or shoving.
19.	Name calling.

Signs of someone abused

1.	Socially isolated and withdrawn.
2.	Considers marriage a prison. The abused spouse may talk in extremes about it, as though it were a perfect or a terrible marriage.
3.	May have been abused as a child or witnessed parents' violence.
4.	May be depressed or suicidal.
5.	Tends to be angry and fearful at the same time.
6.	Wears long sleeved shirts to cover the bruises.
7.	Often denies the seriousness of the problem.
8.	Usually co-dependent and returns to the relationship.
9.	May be apathetic: Low motivation to do anything.
10.	May abuse alcohol, street drugs, and prescriptive medications.
11.	May have nervous habits and poor hygiene.
12.	Talks negatively about herself and life in general.

There is a high relationship between eating disorders and abuse, especially for bulimics and binge eaters. Those abused often turn to food to make them feel safe and nurtured. Some obese people indicate their fat is to protect their internal organs from the physical abuse. The percentage of males who are abusers is greater than female abusers. However, there are also abusive women. The problem is many men are ashamed to admit they allowed a woman to abuse them. Thus, these numbers may be greater than reported.

131

SELF EVALUATION:

1. My personal experience with abusing or being abused.

    a. I grew up being abused and I am repeating the practice.
    b. My parents abused me and now my spouse abuses me.
    c. I abuse to have control.

2. My beliefs regarding abuse:

    a. I deserve to be abused because I am fat.
       (No one deserves to be hit no matter what one's size.)

    b. It is my fault my partner hits me because I do stupid things.
       (There is no excuse for anyone to hit you. You don't deserve to be hit no matter what you do.)

    c. I need to hit in order to be in charge.
       (You will feel better about yourself when you stop hitting and when you find other ways to be in charge.)

3. Action I could take to no longer abuse or be abused:

    a. Talk about what I feel rather than act on it.
    b. Attend Amend or group meetings for abusers (or abused).
    c. Get out of a relationship where there is abuse.
    d. Tell the abuser that I will call the police if I am ever abused again.

4. Fear I have to get out of the abusive relationship:

    a. My abuser said I would be killed.
       (Get help immediately. Call a shelter to get help.)

    b. I will always live in fear that he would find me.
       (Make sure you have a restraining order against him in case you are found.)

    c. My abuser has convinced me that I can't make it on my own.

5. My eating is related to my abuse:

   *a. I refuse to eat after being abused. My eating is the only
       area in my life that no one else can control.(Anorexic)*
   b. I purge after I have been abused. (Bulimic)
   *c. I overeat in order to feel better after I have been abused.
       (Binge eater)*

EXERCISES:

1. Visualize yourself no longer abusing or being in an abusive
   situation. What does that feel like? What changes do you need to
   make? What are you doing in the visualization that you are not
   doing now?

2. Journal your thoughts and feelings about abusive relationships.
   Write a letter to the abuser. You don't have to give the letter to the
   abuser for it to be helpful to you.

3. For additional help, read <u>Battered Woman</u> by Lenore Walker or
   <u>Getting Free: You Can End Abuse and Take Back Your Life</u> by
   Ginny NiCarthy.

How Your Co-dependence/Dependence/ Independence Affect Your Weight and Self-esteem

Co-dependency is when you are more concerned about how someone
else feels rather than your own feelings and thoughts. It is based on the
false belief that your worth and importance is defined outside yourself
and that you can't handle the loss of love. Are you the caretaker? Do you
feel responsible for others' feelings? Do you feel their needs and feelings
are more important than your own? If you do this, the other person
generally becomes resentful of your actions. You imply that she is not
good enough to take care of herself, and you can take care of her better
than she can. It shows lack of respect as well as a need on your part to
feel important. I often see people who say that they don't understand why
a former lover no longer wants anything to do with them. They say, "I

did everything for him." Yes, and he may have felt smothered and it was not what he wanted.

To maintain a healthy relationship with others, we need a combination of having our independent and dependent needs met. Many of my clients indicate they are fearful of becoming dependent for fear they will lose their independence. Certainly, there are some relationships where your partner wishes you would lose your independence and become dependent upon him. However, you don't have to do it! Often the person who doesn't want to be dependent is fearful of intimacy and getting hurt. A balance of independence and dependence is what you want to achieve.

Anorexics tend to appear independent. Most anorexics have a difficult time learning from others and being open-minded because they fear change. They like to do what's familiar and comfortable. Bulimics and binge eaters sometimes are open-minded and easily influenced by others. They tend to be dependent or co-dependent. Male bulimics and binge eaters tend to be more dependent or co-dependent than the general male population.

People often isolate themselves from others so they have more time for their relationship with food. As the relationship with food increases, people often lessen their time with friends, family, and acquaintances. This isolation increases their loneliness and increases their need for food. Loneliness does not have to mean you are isolated. You can be in a marriage and feel alone, but you can also be surrounded by people and feel lonely. A person who is lonely is usually looking for fulfillment outside herself and is expecting someone else to meet her needs. Once you learn to meet your needs in ways other than food, loneliness will be the exception instead of the rule. Your acknowledgement of your own presence will help satisfy your needs. The next time you feel lonely, think of what you enjoy doing alone. Maybe it is reading, watching a movie, going for a walk, or going out to dinner. When you find out what you need, try to fulfill that need.

Anorexics feel lonely and isolated because of their starvation and control. They don't fill their emptiness with food. Bulimics isolate themselves from others so they can purge. Increasing their time with others is helpful to overcome their purging. Binge eaters often spend more time with friends who share their compulsion for food. If eating is the only thing you have in common with your friends, you may want to find friends who enjoy other things.

Men with eating disorders feel especially isolated since little is written for them. Males also don't get support from other males in regard to their disorder, which adds to their isolation. Literature on male eating disorders is like female eating disorder literature was a decade ago.

SELF EVALUATION:

1. **The people in my life that I have co-dependent, dependent, and independent relationships with:**

    a. ***Co-dependent:*** *My husband.*
    b. ***Dependent:*** *My mother.*
    c. ***Independent:*** *My children.*

2. **Ways I am co-dependent:**

    a. Concerned about what others think instead of what I think.
    b. Need to take care of others.
    c. Think about what others are feeling instead of what I feel.
    d. I put my needs last.
    e. I feel responsible for others' actions.
    f. I feel responsible for feelings of other people.

3. **Ways I am dependent:**

    a. Afraid to do things alone.
    b. Financially dependent on spouse.
    c. Need for others' approval.
    d. Afraid to be alone.
    e. I don't trust my own opinion.
    f. I feel as if I can not accomplish anything without checking it out with others.

4. **Ways I am independent:**

    a. Work independently.
    b. Think independently.
    c. Go places alone.
    d. I do not need approval from others.

5. **In what areas of my life do I take care of others?**

    a. Financial: *I support my spouse.*
    b. Emotional: *I try to protect others from getting hurt.*
    c. Sexual: *I have sex when I am not interested in order to please my partner.*
    d. Intellectual: *I help others at work to understand what to do when they are needing help.*
    e. Physically: *I help my invalid mother who lost her sight.*

6. **Do I feel someone other than me is responsible for my feelings? Do I feel that if someone else takes care of me, I will feel happy, lovable, and worthy? If so, I need to change by:**

    a. Taking responsibility for my own actions.
    b. Being more independent.
    c. Learning to take care of my own needs.

7. **How is my behavior overtly controlling as the caretaker?**

    a. Blaming, anger, irritation, righteousness, violence, or explaining.
    b. Accusing, interrogating, lecturing, lying, threatening, or crying.
    c. Silence, tantrums, or withholding.

8. **Beliefs that would be healthier for my independence or dependence needs:**

    a. It is O.K. for me to have both independent and dependent needs.
    (It is not only O.K., but is necessary for good mental health.)

    b. I don't have to be totally dependent on my spouse in order to be a good partner.
    (If you are too dependent, your spouse will resent you.)

    c. If I become dependent, I do not have to give up my independence.

9. **My eating is related to my co-dependency, independence, or dependency:**

   a. *When I am alone, I starve myself to make sure I am in control. (Anorexic)*
   b. *When I feel like I am losing my independence, I purge. (Bulimic)*
   c. *When I feel like I am getting too dependent, I binge. (Binge eater)*

EXERCISES:

1. Visualize yourself having a healthy relationship which encourages a balance of independence and dependence. On a scale of 1-10, how does that feel? What changes do you need to make for this to happen?

2. Journal your thoughts and feelings about your co-dependence, dependence, and independence.

3. For additional help, read <u>Facing Co-dependency</u> by Pia Mellody, or <u>Co-dependent No More</u> by Melodie Beattie, or <u>Co-dependence. Misunderstood-Mistreated</u> by Anne Wilson Schaef.

How Control Issues Affect Your Weight and Self-esteem

Anorexics are in control of their lives, whereas bulimics and binge eaters are out of control. Control is how anorexics define themselves. Anorexics want things done their way. It is difficult for them to let go of their control for fear they will get fat. Anorexics have a difficult time being flexible. Changes for them must be slow. Adding a new food to their limited diet is a big step for them.

Bulimics and binge eaters feel out of control much of the time. When their life is under control, their food becomes controlled. Once the bulimic and the binge eater begin to eat healthy foods and three meals plus one or two snacks, they experience fewer episodes of out-of-control eating.

SELF EVALUATION:

1. **What are the ways I am controlling in my life and with others?**
2. **What are the areas of control in my life that I could let go?**

   a. *Not have to have everything so orderly.*
   b. *Not make the bed in the morning.*
   c. *Not have to weigh myself so often.*
   d. *Not have to have things done my way.*

3. **Beliefs I could have regarding control:**

   a. *I could lessen my control and still not get fat.*
   b. *I can make changes slowly and step-by-step. I do not have to make the changes all at once.*
   c. *I can be in control of my life as well as my eating if I stop and think of how I want to do it.*

4. **How can I structure my eating so I am not out of control?**

   a. *Make sure I eat breakfast, lunch, and dinner.*
   b. *Eat two snacks a day.*
   c. *Eat foods from the different food groups.*

5. **My eating is related to my control:**

   a. *I have lots of control by not eating. (Anorexic)*
   b. *When I feel out of control, I purge. (Bulimics)*
   c. *I overeat because the rest of my life is out of control too. (Bulimic and binge eater)*

EXERCISES:

1. Visualize yourself in control of your life and eating in the way that you desire. Visualize it and then practice it. What are you doing differently in the visualization from what you are doing now? On a scale of 1-10, how does it feel to have your control issues be less of a problem for you?

138

2. Observe others who do not have control issues. What are they doing that you could do? Good luck.

3. Write in your journal thoughts and feelings about your control issues. Indicate what action you can take to make your life easier for you.

4. For additional help, read <u>Hunger So Wide and Deep. American Women Speak Out On Eating Problems</u> by Becky Thompson or <u>The Invisible Woman: Confronting Weight Prejudice in America</u> by Charisse Goodman.

How to Stop the People Pleasing
(Inner vs. Other Directed)

Inner-directed people are able to find happiness within themselves rather than looking for happiness outside themselves. The inner-directed person asks herself what she wants, needs, feels and finds the answers for herself. The other-directed person's worth appears to be whatever others think, want, and need her to accomplish. The problem with pleasing others instead of yourself is you can only assume what another wants. In addition, what may please one may displease another, so you can't win.

People with eating disorders are usually other-directed. Food is one of the avenues outside themselves to help them feel good. Dependence on a scale is an example of a person's worth determined by the number on the scale. If the scale is up, the day is ruined. If the weight is down, the day is good until a celebration with food upsets it. Therefore, it is, better to determine your weight from how you feel, how your clothes fit, and from inner sources rather than outer sources, such as a scale. It was only after I became more inner-directed that I realized what my husband meant when he said, "No matter how much I give to you, it's never enough." I kept wanting more because I was unable to give to myself what I needed. I expected everyone else to give it to me instead.

Anorexics tend to be less likely than bulimics or binge eaters to worry about pleasing others. Men generally are less concerned with what people think than females.

SELF EVALUATION:

1. **People in my life I try to please:**
2. **Examples of when I am inner-directed are:**

   a. *I ask myself what I feel, want, and need.*
   b. *I ask my child within what she needs and wants.*
   c. *Do things alone.*

3. **Examples of when I am other-directed are:**

   a. *Rely on what others think to determine my actions.*
   b. *Dependent on others.*
   c. *Check the scale daily to see what I weigh.*

4. **A problem pleasing others presents for me:**

   a. *I don't have enough time to think of my needs since I am always thinking about what others want from me.*
   b. *What makes some of my friends happy makes others unhappy.*
   c. *It makes me feel empty inside because I am responding to their wishes and not my own.*

5. **Beliefs I could use to help me become more inner-directed and less other-directed:**

   a. *My needs are determined by what I think rather than what others think.*
   b. *The only way to learn to trust my own answers is to start depending on them.*
   c. *My worth is not dependent upon what others think.*

6. **Fears I have in becoming more inner-directed:**

   a. *I will become self-centered and selfish.*
   b. *I will like it and not want to be with people.*
   c. *I will have to deal with my emotions and make my own decisions.*

7. **My eating is related to my lack of inner-directness and pleasing others:**

   a. Since I'm concerned with what others think, I'm not aware of my own body's signals that tell me when and what to eat.
   b. Food is a source of pleasure outside myself.
   c. If I could learn to have more pleasures within myself, I might need less reinforcement outside myself, such as food.

EXERCISES:

1. Interview or observe people who you feel model a sense of inner-direction. Ask how they became this way, how they think and react to situations so you can get a clearer idea of how to change your thinking and ways. What are they doing that you could do?

2. Visualize yourself meeting your needs instead of trying to please others. On a scale of 1-10, how does that feel?

3. Write your thoughts and feelings in regard to your inner vs. outer-directness and pleasing others.

4. For additional help, read Hunger Pains by Mary Pipher.

Set Necessary Boundaries (Who Owns the Problem?)

Lack of boundaries is a common problem of people with eating disorders or addictions, such as alcoholism. Boundary issues are knowing who owns the problem. How often do you get upset when someone else is upset, although it has nothing to do with you? When do you take on responsibility for fixing someone else's problem rather than giving her the right to fix it herself? People with poor boundaries assume responsibility for others and they carry around extra burdens (extra weight).

If you had an intrusive parent, it is probably difficult for you to identify who owns the problem because your parents didn't model this for you. Whenever you feel weighed down with problems, ask yourself whose problems are getting you down? If they aren't your problems, let it go. You will feel lighter, freer, and the other person will be appreciative that you didn't interfere.

An anorexic's mother often has poor boundaries because she is so enmeshed with her daughter that she doesn't allow her daughter to be independent. When the child hurts, the mother hurts too. Such daughters often complain they have nothing of their own, including their own pain.

Bulimics and binge eaters often have boundary problems similar to the alcoholic family. Family members believe they are responsible for the person with the eating disorder. This allows the addicted person to escape responsibility for her own actions. When we don't take responsibility for our own actions, we blame others. Remember when you point your finger at another, you have three fingers pointing back at yourself. The things we don't like about others are often the same things that we don't like about ourselves. So the next time you blame someone, ask why it bothers you so much.

SELF EVALUATION:

1. **My issues of confusion with my boundaries:**

   a. I allow my mother to be intrusive.
   b. I am intrusive in my children's lives.
   c. I feel it is my job to make everybody happy.

2. **My boundary issues began when:**

   a. I was responsible for younger siblings.
   b. My family used to make excuses for my alcoholic father.
   c. I tried to make everything O.K. for my spouse.

3. **People who do not respect my boundaries and ways they don't respect it:**

   *a. **Mother-in-law:** When she invites herself to go on vacation with my husband and me.*
   *b. **Mother:** Wants to know all about my sex life with my spouse.*
   *c. **Children:** Come into our bedroom when the door is closed.*

142

4. **Beliefs that would be helpful in setting necessary boundaries:**

   a. *I need to allow my children to learn from their mistakes.*
   b. *My spouse is responsible for his own actions.*
   c. *I am responsible for my actions, not others' actions.*
   d. *If I spend energy fixing my own problems and allow others to resolve their problems, I will feel less overwhelmed.*

5. **My fears in allowing others to resolve their own problems:**

   a. *Afraid I will lose some power I have when involved in others' lives.*
   b. *I am afraid I will not be needed.*
   c. *Afraid I will have no friends.*

6. **My boundary problems influence my eating by:**

   a. *When I don't set limits with people, I get mad at them and stuff this feeling with food. (Bulimics and Binge eaters)*
   b. *I sense others' disapproval, but I don't know what is wrong so I eat.*
   c. *When I take on others' responsibilities, I feel overwhelmed so I eat to comfort me.*

EXERCISES:

1. Visualize yourself not taking on others' problems as your own. What is a problem that you could let go? Let go of one situation Then practice letting go of another. Begin with one in which you will succeed. On a scale of 1-10, how does this feel?

2. Journal thoughts and feelings about setting appropriate boundaries and letting go of others' problems. After writing, underline with one colored pen when you are setting appropriate boundaries. With a different colored pen, indicate when you aren't setting boundaries.

3. For additional help, read Where You End & I Begin by Anne Katherine or Boundaries and Relationships-Knowing, Protecting, and Enjoying Self by Charles Whitefield.

Develop Support Systems

We all need support. When you feel you can do everything by yourself and don't need others, you rob yourself of an important aspect of life. You are not weak when you ask for help. In fact, you are being a normal intelligent human being. You are weak if you always ask for help without trying things on your own, but there are times each of us needs help. It is important to know when to work things out for yourself and when to ask for help.

Friends can be one of the biggest support systems you have to help you overcome your eating disorder. It is important to find friends who understand your problem, but don't enable you. For example, if all your friends purge with you, you want to find friends who have something in common other than purging. Friends accept you for who you are without trying to change you. They love you for being you. It is difficult to give up the relationship you have with food if you don't have any friends.

Anorexics have a difficult time forming friendships and allowing others to support them. They feel they're strong enough to take care of themselves. They don't want anyone to change their lives. Bulimics and binge eaters also find it difficult to ask for support. They are more likely to give support than to receive it. Since men generally don't have the same support from friends as females, they often feel alone with their eating disorder.

It may be helpful for you to find a therapist to help you treat your eating disorder. A therapist allows you to solve your situation in a supportive, non-judgmental atmosphere. It allows you to have an objective person help you find answers to your problems. Make sure they are state-licensed and have experience working with people with an eating disorder. It is helpful to ask for referrals from friends who have had positive experiences with a particular therapist.

An eating disorder group is especially helpful because you will see others experience similar issues with their weight and food that you do. It also gives you an opportunity to see the likeable qualities other people with eating disorders possess. This helps you realize that you have value too. As a result, you change the image of yourself.

Anorexics rarely want to join groups because of their competitiveness and fear that they will not be the thinnest. Bulimics and binge eaters generally enjoy groups and derive many benefits from being in a group. It is usually more difficult for males to join eating disorder groups. They aren't used to sharing their problems and a group is often threatening. Some females also find it threatening to have males in their groups.

Overeaters Anonymous may be helpful for you. The advantages of these meetings are they are free, held numerous times a week, and are located at several locations. If you don't feel comfortable with a particular group, find another group. The American Heart Association provides Slim For Life Classes, which can help you eat in a healthy way.

Many people get support from the Internet. People with eating disorders like it because size and weight make no difference to people who use the Internet. People feel safe because they can practice to be assertive, speak their mind, and say what they might not feel comfortable saying face to face. There is also much information and support for people with food and weight issues on the World Wide Web. (See appendix for list of eating disorder support groups on the Internet.)

Friends can also provide different support. It is best to not expect a friend to fulfill all your needs, but it is likely that one friend may provide laughter and another friend will be there for you in crisis. The following are different types of friends to meet your different social needs.

1. Friends in my life who provide **INTIMACY**. (People who provide closeness, warmth, and acceptance. You can express your opinions and feelings, even when they differ from your friend's views. People you can trust and are accessible to you.)

2. Friends in my life with whom I can **SHARE**. (People in the same situation that you are in or who strive for the same goals. People with whom you can share experiences and they share with you as well.)

3. Friends in my life who provide **ASSISTANCE**. (People who provide services or resources for you. People you can depend upon during a crisis.)

4. Friends in my life who provide **GUIDANCE**. (People who provide advice and ways to solve your problems. They help you to take steps to reach your goals.)

5. Friends in my life who provide **CHALLENGE**. (People who make you think, question your reasoning, and who help you to grow.)

6. Friends in my life with whom I can **PLAY and HAVE FUN**. (People with whom you have fun, make you laugh, and enjoy your sense of humor.)

7. Friends in my life who **ACCEPT MY FEELINGS. (**People who acknowledge how you feel and don't try to discount your feelings.)

8. Friends in my life from whom I receive **PHYSICAL CONTACT**. (Persons who give you hugs, affection, and accept your affection.)

9. Friends in my life who are my **TEACHERS**. (People you have contact with who can help you learn more about life, events, and yourself by observing their behaviors.)

SELF EVALUATION:

1. **Do I have friends from each of the types of friends listed above? What type of friends do I need in my life?**

    a. *I need more friends who make me laugh.*
    b. *I need more intimacy with my friends.*
    c. *I need a friend who accepts me for who I am, not how she wants me to be.*
    d. *I need more friends to share my interests.*

2. **Reaction I got as a child when I asked for support:**

    a. *Figure it out for yourself.*
    b. *Only weak people need help from others.*
    c. *I'm busy, what is wrong with you that you can't figure this out?*

3. **How did my family model asking for support?**

    a. *My mother asked everyone for help, which turned me off and I swore I would never be like her.*
    b. *My father said don't ask anyone for help because you will be obligated to them.*
    c. *My siblings laughed at me when I asked for help.*

146

4. **My fears in getting support:**

    a. *I am afraid a therapist won't understand me.*
      (If this happens, you need to find a different therapist.)

    b. *I am afraid to join a group because I'm not comfortable talking about myself.*
      (See a therapist with whom you are comfortable. This may be a first step for you before joining a group.)

    c. *What if I become like my neighbor who goes to O.A. meetings five days a week?*
      (You are in charge of when and how often you go. Maybe your neighbor feels a need at this point in her life for that much support.)

5. **My eating is related to my lack of support:**

    a. *Because I have no support, I feel alone and starve myself to try to get people to help. (Anorexic)*
      (Perhaps it would be better for you to ask for the help you want rather than starving yourself.)

    b. *When I have no support, I purge more. (Bulimic)*
      (It becomes a vicious cycle. The less support, the more isolated, the more you purge.)

    c. *When I have no support, I binge more. (Bulimic and binge eater)*

EXERCISES:

1. Visualize yourself surrounded by all the support you need. Feel the warmth and love of all these people. Enjoy them. Allow their support to enter into your being. How have you surrounded yourself differently in this visualization than you do in your daily life?

2. Journal thoughts and feelings about getting support. What action do you need to take to get the support you desire?

3. For additional help, read <u>Treating Eating Disorders</u> by Werne and Yalom, or <u>Beauty Myth: How Images of Beauty are Used Against Women</u> by Naomi Wolf,or <u>Group Psychotherapy for Eating Disorders</u> by Harper-Giuffre and MacKenzie.

Social Evaluation

NEEDS	CAUSES (1-10)	ACTION TO TAKE (1-10)
Let go of the past.	*Parents not there for me. (3)*	*Write my parents a letter telling how I feel until my resentment is gone. (8)*
Develop healthy relationships.	*I am scared I will get hurt. (2)*	*Tell myself it is better to have loved and lost than to have never loved. (7)*
Intimacy	*I don't know how to be intimate. (2)*	*Get a pet and learn from my pet. (9)*
Vulnerability	*I don't let anyone know me. (2)*	*Share feelings with my best friend. (8)*
Control	*My way or the highway. (1)*	*Be more open-minded. (8)*

NEEDS	CAUSES (1-10)	ACTION TO TAKE (1-10)
Co-dependency	*I think of what others feel, need, and want.* (4)	*Think of my feelings, wants, and needs instead of taking care of others.* (9)
Dependent	*I am financially dependent on my spouse.* (3)	*I can get a part-time job so that I don't feel so dependent on my partner.* (8)
Independent	*I am so independent that I do not let others get close to me.* (3)	*Ask for help from others.* (8)
People Pleasing	*I lead my life trying to please others.* (2)	*Start thinking of pleasing me instead of everyone else.* (9)
Expectations of Others	*I expect people to react in a certain way and then I get disappointed when they don't react that way.* (2)	*Allow others to be how they want to be instead of how I want them to respond.* (8)

NEEDS	CAUSES (1-10)	ACTION TO TAKE (1-10)
Boundary Issues	*I don't know what my problem is from others.* *(2)*	*I don't need to feel responsible for taking care of others. That's their job not mine.* *(9)*
Loneliness and Isolation	*I don't have any friends.* *(1)*	*Find some new interests and go where others share the same interest.* *(9)*

CHAPTER FIVE

Improve Your Self-esteem to Change Your Weight

The psychological self includes self-esteem, identity, and personality. When we try to be something we're not, we mess with our psyches and self-esteem. You can't expect a daisy to become a tulip any more than you can expect to be an unnatural weight. People with eating disorders do this often. Their body is one shape and size. They try to make it a different size. The result is frustration, anger, and a poor self-concept. If you can accept your natural size, a healthy psychological self emerges.

Your self-esteem is tied to your confidence in yourself. How fortunate you are if your family members told you that you could achieve whatever you desired. Their belief in you helped you to believe in yourself. Likewise, if you were told that you'd never amount to anything, you'll believe that too, unless you use this to motivate yourself to prove they were wrong.

When I was in high school a school counselor told me I shouldn't attempt to go to college because I would fail. I was confused. Teachers and others told me I had great potential. I received many awards and scholarships. Yet, I never forgot his words and the impact it had on me. I had to prove to myself that I could achieve. It was such a pleasure when I went back to a basketball game at my high school and this counselor asked me what I was doing. I proudly said, "I am teaching at the university." It gave me great pleasure to prove him wrong.

■■■

An anorexic damages her psychic energies when she does anything and everything to become thin. When her energies are all used up for this goal, there is no energy left for anything else. Her physical self fights starvation, but she doesn't listen.

Bulimics and binge eaters need to look at their psychological selves to see how their preoccupation with food and weight denies other parts of themselves. When they enlarge their view of themselves to more than their weight, they expand and enrich their self-esteem. Just as females need to accept their bodies as being larger than they desire, males need to accept their bodies as being smaller than they wish.

How to Improve Your Self-esteem

Your self-esteem is how you feel about yourself. Is your self-esteem determined by how you look, how much you weigh, or what you are wearing? If your weight goes down, does your self-esteem go up? Or if your weight goes up, does your self-esteem go down? If this is true, your self-esteem is like a roller coaster, going up and down, providing little stability to your self-worth. When your self-esteem is based on factors such as weight, what others think, and when you get or don't get approval, you set yourself up for mood swings. These external factors provide little stability and a poor self-esteem.

Self-esteem provides stability. You don't have control over how you grew up, but this is where you formed your self-image. As an adult, however, you have the power to undo or redo your self-image by taking control of your self-esteem. Self-esteem is about being on your own side. It is the belief in yourself and being your own best friend. There is no one in the entire world like you. Rejoice in your uniqueness. It is your right and privilege to feel good about being you.

Anorexics often appear to be self-confident, assured, and have a healthy self-esteem. They are smart, attractive, and appear to have everything going for them. But inside they feel lonely, lost, frustrated, and imprisoned within their body. It is important to them to hide how terrible they feel. Since they don't like themselves, they're sure others will reject them, if their real self is known.

152

Bulimics' self-esteem is improved when they are able to stop purging. Purging makes bulimics hate themselves and lowers their self-esteem. Binge eaters identify themselves with how much weight they have gained. When their self-esteem isn't determined by what they weigh, they are less frustrated with their weight.

SELF EVALUATION:

1. **Ways I look for my self-esteem from others:**

     a. *From what others say about me.*
     b. *What I think others think.*
     c. *Comparing myself to others.*

2. **Factors influencing my self-esteem are:**

     a. *Parents loving or not loving me.*
     b. *Siblings, parents, and friends' comments.*
     c. *Rewards or lack of them from work or school.*
     d. *My negative talk about myself.*

3. **Other ways my self-esteem is determined besides my looks:**

     a. *Contributions I make to society.*
     b. *Type of family member I am: Wife, husband, mother, father, daughter, son.*
     c. *Friend.*
     d. *Job strengths.*

4. **Ways I could improve my self-esteem:**

     a. *Be more positive rather than critical in my self-talk.*
     b. *Be more honest, appreciative, conscientious.*
     c. *Treat others and myself the way I would like to be treated.*
     d. *Eat healthier.*
     e. *Exercise less. (Anorexic)*
     f. *Exercise more. (Bulimic or Binge eater)*

5. My eating is related to my self-esteem:

> *a. When I don't eat, I feel better about myself. (Anorexic)*
> *b. When I purge, my self-esteem goes down. (Bulimic)*
> *c. The lower my weight, the higher my self-esteem.*

EXERCISES:

1. Take a time in your life when you felt the best you ever felt about yourself. Let the confidence and enjoyment resurface in your life today. What was the situation where you felt the most confident and your self-esteem was the highest?

2. Write in your journal thoughts and feelings about your self-esteem and things you can do to improve it. Identify where you want to start and where you want to be. Then take small steps to get there.

3. For additional help, read <u>Self-esteem: Tools for Recovery</u> by Hall and Cohen or <u>Self-esteem </u>by McKay and Fanning.

Steps for a Healthy Self-esteem

1. I accept the kid in me and will allow her to be present. When I acknowledge the child within, she will have less need to sneak out and eat abusively.
2. I will be a caretaker, not a critic to the little girl in me who wants to eat unhealthy foods or amounts. I will offer her diversions so that my kid need not rebel.
3. I will accept and acknowledge my feelings and needs. I will not judge my feelings, but accept and express them instead of using food to sedate myself.
4. I will eat slowly, taking time to see, smell, and taste my food.
5. I will accept my body today rather than wait to accept it at its ideal weight.

6.	I will plan frequent non-food rewards and fun. These fun outlets will help lessen my turning to food for entertainment, amusement, or fun.
7.	I will ask for strokes, build support systems, and seek warm fuzzy people and situations. These strokes will lessen my need to use food for emotional reasons.
8.	I will count my successes and strengths, rather than looking at my weaknesses to determine who I am and how I feel about myself.
9.	Relaxation and meditation time will be part of my life style.
10.	Exercise thirty minutes five times a week.
11.	I will not blame others for my eating problems and will take responsibility for what I eat.
12.	I will let go of my past as a problem, enjoy the present, and look forward to the future.
13.	I will change my thinking from looking at the negative to looking at the positive.
14.	I will set realistic goals for myself so that I will have successes.
15.	I will be assertive in asking for what I want and need. I will express these needs to others and myself.
16.	I will view myself as more than what I weigh to include all aspects of my life.

For additional help, read Self-esteem Comes in All Sizes by Carol Johnson, Self-esteem by Nathaniel Brandon, or One Size Does Not Fit All by Beverly Naidus.

How to Develop Self-Love
Without Being Selfish or Selfless

It is important to distinguish self-love from selfishness. This is an important concept to understand in order to overcome your eating disorder, yet it is one that is often misunderstood. To love yourself is to be, kind, compassionate, loving, and caring for you. It doesn't interfere with anybody else's wants or needs. Self-love is behavior that has no ill effect on another person. Selfishness is when you fulfill your needs and are insensitive as to how your behavior affects anyone else. It often results in hurting others.

Sometimes there is a fine line as to when behavior is self-love or selfish, but generally not. You can't love another unless you first love yourself. Selfish people don't love themselves because if they loved themselves, they would also be sensitive to others. If you are a self-less person, not only do you not love yourself, but you also appear to have hollowness about you. Others say, "Hello, is anybody home? Is there anything happening inside you?"

Anorexics' starvation isn't a sign of self-love, but rather self-deprivation. Since the anorexic is consumed with not being fat and not eating, she often doesn't have the energy to think about how her behavior affects others. My experience is that anorexics are people who love, but are temporarily stuck in their preoccupation with themselves. Once they can get past the sole thought of their weight, they tend to be sensitive and considerate people.

Bulimics and binge eaters are rarely selfish and are usually the opposite. They often appear self-less and will do anything for others. They are generally sensitive and intuitive people who can't think of their own needs because they are too busy worrying about pleasing others.

Men with eating disorders generally appear to be less selfish than the general male population. They tend to be sensitive and aware of what others are feeling, even though they may not be aware of their own feelings.

SELF EVALUATION:

1. Ways I am selfish:

   a. *I am inconsiderate of others' feelings, wants, or needs.*
   b. *I don't go to my children's activities because I am playing golf, shopping, or doing what I want to do for me.*
   c. *I spend so much money on junk food I don't have enough money to buy my children the shoes that they need.*
   d. *I tell my family if I can't eat where I want to eat, I won't go out to dinner with them.*

2. Ways I am self-less:

    a. I will buy my children new clothes they don't need, yet I haven't bought myself any new clothes in the past five years.

    b. I am always so busy doing for others I have no time to do the things I like to do, such as reading a book.

    c. When I allow others to walk all over me, I feel bad about myself.

    d. I consider others' needs instead of my own.

3. Ways I show self-love:

    a. Asking myself what I feel, need, and want and then responding to it.

    b. Being kind and generous and caring of myself.

    c. I get a baby sitter each week so I can go to a movie, art museum or whatever I want so I can have some quality time for myself.

    d. I buy myself a new outfit when I see something I like.

4. Fears I have about loving myself:

    a. I will become like my selfish uncle who nobody likes. All he ever thinks about is himself.
    (Self-loving people are not selfish nor do they only think about themselves.)

    b. That I won't have enough time to give to my family or to my friends.
    (If you don't meet your own needs, you won't be able to meet others' needs.)

    c. I'm afraid that I'll go overboard and be insensitive to others.
    (At first you may go overboard. Many people do. It feels good to take care of yourself. At first you may be insensitive to others. However, you will soon realize that it doesn't feel good to be this way and you will learn to balance your needs with others. Try it, you'll like it.)

157

5. Beliefs that I have about loving myself:

   a. It is difficult to love myself when I hate my body so much.
   (When you learn to love yourself, you will stop being critical of your body. This doesn't mean you have to continue to stay at your present weight. It does mean love yourself and your body no matter what your weight.)

   b. I can't love myself unless others love me first.
   (You have this backwards. No one is going to love you until you love yourself.)

   c. It is difficult to change from hating myself to loving myself when all I ever heard from my family is how awful I am.
   (Yes, it is difficult for you to make this change, but you can and when you do, you will feel much better.)

6. My eating affects my lack of self-love:

   a. When I feel bad about myself, I starve myself. (Anorexic)
   b. When I hate myself, I binge. (Bulimic and binge eater)
   c. It is difficult to love myself when I do not eat healthy.

EXERCISES:

1. Each time you go through a doorway say, "I am lovable." As the saying goes, "Fake it until you make it." Then continue to say, "I love myself. I think I am a pretty neat person."

2. Wear a rubber band and each time you say a negative statement about yourself, snap the band. Then change the negative statement to a loving, affirming statement.

3. Visualize yourself loving yourself. What are you doing in your visualization that you could incorporate in your life now? On a scale of 1-10, how does that feel?

4. Journal thoughts and feelings you have in regard to self-love, selfishness, and selflessness. Underline each with a different colored pen so you can chart your progress.

5. For additional help, read <u>Appetites: On Search for True Nourishment</u> by Geneen Roth or <u>How to be Your Own Best Friend</u> by Newman, Mildred & Bernard Berkowitz.

Love the Parent, Adult, and Child Within

We all have a parent, adult, and child ego states within us. There is the adult, the grown-up who makes wise decisions for us, who is the rational part of ourselves. We have both a critical parent and a nurturing parent inside. The critical parent sends messages that we aren't good enough. This may or may not be the same messages your parents sent you as a child. The nourishing parent is warm, loving, and tender to the child within us.

Think of the child within as a flower. Once the seed is planted, she needs to be nurtured, loved, and accepted. She wants to play, be spontaneous, have fun, and enjoy life. It is the child within who wants a cookie now and does not want to wait. The adult can ask if you are hungry. If not, ask your child within to wait until you are hungry before having the cookie. It is the critical parent who says, "There you go again wanting a cookie when you aren't even hungry." It is the nurturing parent who says she will comfort you so you don't need a cookie.

If you are anorexic, you are in touch with your critical parent, but you don't let your nurturing parent be present. Your critical thinking has beaten down your child. This adult is probably very alive in you because you rule by your reasoning. If you are bulimic or a binge eater, you are nurturing to others, but not to yourself. Try to nurture yourself in the same way you nurture others. The critical parent tends to overrule the nurturing parent in you. Too often this parent squelches the child with food rather than listening to what the child really needs.

Males with an eating disorder often do not allow their child within to play. They may also be critical of themselves turning to food for relief from their own criticism.

SELF EVALUATION:

1. What do I need to do for my parent, adult and child?

a. I need to learn to love my child within.

b. I can stop allowing my critical parent to be so judgmental. I want to nurture my child within. When I do this for myself, I won't have to be angry or disappointed that I didn't get this from my parents. I can give it to myself.

c. I can depend on my adult within to help me be rational and make wise decisions.

2. What does my child want to do, say, or need?

a. My child within wants to tell my critical parent to stop hurting me. I don't deserve to be constantly criticized.

b. My child within wants to play and have fun--something I never got to do when I was a child.

c. My child within needs all the same things I needed when I was a child--to be loved, nurtured, appreciated and valued.

3. What does my critical parent do, say or need?

a. My critical parent says I don't want to be like this, but it's all I know.

b. My critical parent inside me is acting like I was treated by my parents.

c. My critical parent needs to be replaced by my nurturing and loving parent.

4. What does my nurturing parent do, say, or need?

a. My nurturing parent says I want to give you all the love, comfort and support you deserve.

b. My nurturing parent needs my child within to accept the love and praise she deserves.

c. My nurturing parent wants to replace my critical parent.

160

5. What does my adult do, say, or need?

   a. *My adult says that she will give me answers and help me remain logical if I will allow her to be heard.*
   b. *My adult needs the opportunity to be able to speak and have my inner child listen.*
   c. *My adult wants to have my nurturing parent ask her for advice when she needs it.*

6. My eating is related to my critical parent within:

   a. *When my critical parent is present, I rebel and stop eating. (Anorexic)*
   b. *My critical parent makes me feel like purging. (Bulimic)*
   c. *My critical parent makes me feel bad about myself. Consequently, I overeat. (Binge eater)*

7. My eating is related to my nurturing parent within:

   a. *I get scared when my nurturing parent tries to nurture me, so I starve myself more. (Anorexic)*
   b. *I don't believe I deserve my nurturing parent to care for me, so I purge. (Bulimic)*
   c. *I overeat when my nurturing parent tries to care for me. I don't know how to respond to such care and love since it is so new to me. (Binge eater)*

8. My eating is related to my adult within:

   a. *I get tired of hearing my adult within (my rational voice) tell me what to do, so I starve to rebel.(Anorexic)*
   b. *If I would listen to my adult within (my rational voice), it would help me with my purging.(Bulimic)*
   c. *If I would listen to my adult within (my rational voice), it would help me with my emotional eating. (Binge eater)*
   d. *I rebel against my adult (my rational voice) because I get tired of being responsible, rational, and predictable.*

161

9. My eating is related to my child within:

    a. *I don't allow my child within to play because I fear I would lose control. (Anorexic)*
    b. *I allow my child within to eat whenever and whatever she wants. (Bulimic and binge eater)*
    c. *My child within wants me to nurture and care for her.*
    d. *My child within wants to be naughty and eat lots of unhealthy foods.*

EXERCISES:

1. Close your eyes and relax. Imagine that child inside yourself. There is a child in you who wants to play, wants you to stop criticizing her, and wants to have her needs met. Listen to the child who says, "I am tired of being good and doing for others. I want my needs heard." Now imagine the parent inside of you. See the critical parent who says mean and nasty things to that child of yours. Take that critical parent and say, "NO MORE! I am not going to let you hurt my child anymore." Stamp out the critical parent with your feet. Eliminate it. Now substitute your critical parent with a nurturing parent who allows you to make mistakes, loves you unconditionally and is always there to protect you from that critical parent. Now say, "Hello" to the adult in you who helps the child within to make decisions that are healthy for you. Thank your adult for helping make decisions the child within does not have the experience to make. Allow yourself to feel this child, nurturing parent, and adult within.

2. Visualize your inner child being nurtured by your nurturing parent. On a scale of 1-10, how does that feel? What action do you need to take to make this happen?

3. Journal the thoughts and feelings you have in regard to loving your parent, adult, and child within. Go back and underline the child, critical parent, nurturing parent, and adult statements with different colored pens. This will help you become aware of your statements. You can chart your progress by having less critical parent comments.

4. For additional help, read, <u>Full Lives: Women Who Have Freed Themselves from Food and Weight Obsession</u> by Lindsey Hall, <u>I'm O.K. You're O.K.</u> by Thomas Harris, <u>An Action Plan for Your Inner Child: Parenting Each Other</u> by Laurie Weiss, or <u>Healing the Child Within</u> by Charles L. Whitfied.

Just Be
(Enjoy the Present)

So often we try to be something we are not. We try to win the approval of others, to meet parents' expectations, and to make ourselves better. There are times we do need to strive to improve, but it is equally important to enjoy the present and accept ourselves. When you allow yourself to be, you accept yourself.

Many of my clients think at first that if they practice this, they will eat like there is no tomorrow. Enjoying the present doesn't mean you won't enjoy tomorrow. It means enjoy the food as you eat it (stay in the present). Thus, you will not need to overeat.

Anorexics have a difficult time enjoying the present because of the high pressure they put on themselves. It is difficult to be in the present when you starve yourself. Anorexics are constantly consumed with the idea of becoming thinner and when they don't eat and are weak, it becomes difficult to enjoy the present.

Bulimics can't enjoy the present because of their purging. Although it gives them relief, it does not bring them pleasure. So much of their time is spent thinking of ways to change their bingeing and purging that it is difficult to enjoy the present.

Often, binge eaters can't accept their being in the present because they feel they have to lose weight in order to enjoy life. Once they can learn to enjoy the present, they probably will lose weight.

SELF EVALUATION:

1. **Past which haunts me and keeps me from enjoying the present:**
2. **Future plans which prevent me from enjoying the present:**
3. **Reasons for not enjoying the present:**

4. **Beliefs I could use to help me in the present:**

   a. *Enjoy today by being myself.*
   b. *Do not put off tomorrow what I can do today.*
   c. *I have only one life to live so I am going to live it the best way I know how.*

5. **My fears about enjoying the present:**

   a. *Afraid I will eat excessively.*
   b. *I feel I am not good enough now and if I start accepting myself I might not change.*
      (To like yourself the way you are now doesn't mean you can't change to better yourself.)

6. **My eating is related to my not enjoying the present:**

   a. *It is difficult to enjoy life when I deprive myself so much. (Anorexic)*
   b. *I would enjoy the present much more if I could stop purging. (Bulimic)*
   c. *If I would enjoy the present, I wouldn't have to overeat like I now do. (Binge eater)*

7. **Action I could take to enjoy the present and not sabotage myself with food:**

   a. *Give myself choices.*
   b. *Stop depriving myself and think of abundance.*
   c. *Stop the critical thinking.*
   d. *Do things I enjoy.*

EXERCISES:

1. Visualize yourself enjoying the present instead of worrying about the past or future. On a scale of 1-10, how does that feel? What is your first step in doing this?

2. Journal feelings and thoughts you have in regard to enjoying the present.

3. For additional help, read <u>Reviving Ophelia: Saving the Selves of Adolescent Girls</u> by Mary Pipher.

Identity to Include More Than What You Weigh

If you make the comment your identity is what you weigh, then I encourage you to re-evaluate that statement. It is sad when you determine your worth only by how you look, how much you weigh, or how small your hips are. What would you think of a friend or associate who felt how she looked was the most important thing in her life? She wouldn't be a very interesting person or a good friend, would she? Yet, is that not what you do to yourself? Maybe you could be more interesting, less inhibited, and feel liberated if you stop obsessing about your weight.

When you become obsessed with your weight, you probably don't see or feel those wonderful qualities you possess. Do you hear and listen to positive things others say about you, such as what a good friend, wife, daughter, or worker you are? Do you think only if you could lose 5, 15, 100 or 250 pounds, you would be a better friend, wife, daughter, or worker? Does your friend insist you lose your desired weight before she likes you? If so, maybe you need a new friend. As the saying goes, with friends like that, who needs enemies? Treat yourself as your own best friend. You deserve to be treated that way.

SELF EVALUATION:

1. **What is my identity?**
2. **What are the beliefs and thoughts that cause me to feel as if my identity is tied to my looks?**

   a. *The only thing that lovers look for is how I look.*
   b. *If I don't have my identity wrapped up in how I look, I'll get fat.*
   c. *This is what my mother modeled for me.*

165

3. **What thoughts do I need to change to feel better about myself and have a healthier identity?**

   a. *I am more than what I weigh.*
   b. *I need to value the other aspects of my life as much as I value my looks.*
   c. *Just because I expand my identity beyond how I look doesn't mean my appearance is not important.*

4. **What are my fears in making this change?**

   a. *I will get fat because I won't care.*
      (No one is suggesting you don't care.)

   b. *There is nothing else important for me to feel good about myself except my weight.*
      (Try to find some other interests so your weight doesn't have to be such an issue for you.)

   c. *I'm afraid I'll disappoint my significant other.*
      (How is that?)

5. **What action could I take in making this change?**

   a. *Praise myself for things I do well besides controlling my weight.*
   b. *Develop other interests and hobbies so that I have more than my weight to think about.*
   c. *Think about my strengths instead of dwelling on all my weaknesses.*

EXERCISES:

1. Visualize yourself making a change in your identity. You want to see yourself to be more than your weight. What is the first step you make? On a scale of 1-10, how does that feel? Good luck in making this change.

2. Write in your journal your thoughts and feelings you have about your identity.

3. For additional help, read <u>The Hungry Self. Women, Eating and Identity</u> by Kim Chernin

Psychological Evaluation

BEHAVIOR	USUAL PATTERN (1-10)	ACTION TO TAKE (1-10)
Self-esteem	*My self-esteem is lowest when others put me down.* *(1)*	*Have what I think be as important as what others think.* *(9)*
Self-love	*I don't ever love myself.* *(1)*	*Treat myself like I am my best friend.* *(9)*
Selfish	*I think only about what I want even when it hurts others.* *(2)*	*I can be more sensitive to others' feelings.* *(8)*
Selfless	*I do not think of my needs, wants, or feelings.* *(1)*	*I can speak up for what I want, need, and feel.* *(9)*

BEHAVIOR	USUAL PATTERN (1-10)	ACTION TO TAKE (1-10)
Critical Parent Within	*I put myself down.* *(1)*	*Change my critical parent to a nurturing parent* *(9)*
Nurturing Parent Within	*I never nurture myself.* *(1)*	*Continue nurturing others, but nurture myself too.* *(9)*
Child Within	*I want to eat now. I have poor impulse control.* *(2)*	*Allow the rational self to speak to my child within.* *(8)*
Adult Within	*I am irrational in my thinking. I respond emotionally, making me feel out of control.* *(1)*	*My rational self can help me like myself and not feel so out of control.* *(9)*
Identity	*My weight and looks determine how I feel about myself.* *(3)*	*My identity includes more than my weight.* *(9)*
Enjoy the present	*I worry about the past and the future.* *(2)*	*Enjoy today.* *(9)*

C H A P T E R   S I X

Enhance Your Spirituality to Change Your Weight and Self-esteem

*W*hen you get in touch with the spiritual aspect of yourself, it may help you overcome your eating problems. The spiritual part of you includes your values, beliefs and a higher power. When you feel like eating for emotional reasons rather than physical reasons, turn to your spirituality. It can provide some of the same inner fullness that food provides. Some people find it is helpful to give thanks to a higher power before a meal. When you fill your insides spiritually, there is less need to fill it with food for emotional reasons.

I am thankful my mother and father instilled a strong faith in me. Both my parents modeled their belief in God. After my father died, my mother inspired me with her example of how she continued to allow God to lead her to a fulfilling life.

Sometimes anorexics, bulimics, and binge eaters find it difficult to get in touch with their spiritual self because they feel their higher power has let them down. Otherwise, they wouldn't have their eating and weight problems. Sometimes they use so much energy to control their weight, they have less energy to get in touch with their spiritual selves.

■■■

Higher Power

It is helpful for most people with eating disorders to have faith in someone other than themselves to help them with their eating problems. Faith is an important aspect of Overeaters Anonymous meetings, based on a twelve-step program. Whether your higher power is God, someone you know, nature, or another belief, it can give you a feeling of hopefulness when you feel hopeless. When you feel hopeless, you feel you don't have the answers for yourself. When you can ask for help from a higher power, you can sometimes receive answers to your questions. You can receive strength by allowing your higher power to help you handle your eating problems in a more successful way.

I have watched my clients' faces show signs of relief when they feel blocked or overwhelmed and use a "God" or "higher power" bag. When they feel stuck on an issue, they write their problem and put it and their feelings into a bag. When they do this, they then let their higher power take care of the issue. They release some of the tension and turmoil of constantly thinking about it. This often allows them to find their own answers even if not right away. When people can trust that the answers will come, they feel comfort rather than anguish. Below is an example of a dialogue a client used which was helpful to her:

Self: *Higher power, please help me to learn from my binge so that I can give up this practice. I hate bingeing, yet I continue to do it. Please help me. I feel so alone and it feels terrible. Please give me the strength to stop.*

Higher Power: *It takes faith to talk to me and ask for my help. That may be what you need to do so you do not have to have a binge. Congratulate yourself for talking to me instead of bingeing. I would always like to be there for you if you would let me.*

Anorexics often have a difficult time staying in touch with their higher power because they fear they will lose control and give up their power. Sometimes bulimics and binge eaters feel as if their higher power has let them down. They may have to let go of this anger before they can allow their higher power back into their lives.

170

SELF EVALUATION:

1. My definition of higher power is someone:

    a. I can ask for help in making decisions.
    b. Who can give me guidance when I ask for it.
    c. Who gives me extra strength knowing this power is always present.

2. My fear in having a higher power is:

    a. It will mean I will have less power.
    (You will actually feel more power because you have released stressed energy.)

    b. It will make me weird.
    (Because you know one person with a higher power who is weird doesn't mean all are weird.)

    c. It may inhibit me from doing things I would like to do.
    (It may free you up to be able to do more things.)

3. My beliefs that prevent me from having a higher power:

    a. I can't trust myself; why would I trust someone else?
    (Higher power may help you to learn to trust yourself.)

    b. It is a sign of weakness to rely on a higher power.
    (You will probably feel stronger.)

    c. It is important for me to be in complete control of myself at all times.

4. My higher power could help me with my eating:

    a. I surrender to my higher power when I feel powerless.
    b. I speak to my higher power before I overeat and ask for guidance.
    c. I write to my higher power to get answers to my problems.

EXERCISES:

1. Take the last time you had a binge. Turn to your higher power for help. Have a dialogue with your higher power in regard to this binge. What would you say to your higher power? What would your higher power say to you? Write this in your journal or talk to an empty chair, pretending your higher power is in the chair. You can continue to have such a dialogue about any problems you have.

2. Take a brown paper bag and write "higher power" or "God bag" on it. The next time you feel discouraged or do not know what to do, write this problem down on a piece of paper. Place the paper and all the feelings in the bag with the problem. State to your higher power, "I am no longer able to deal with this problem. I give it to you to handle this for me."

3. Visualize yourself having a higher power that guides and supports you. What would you like this higher power to be like? Allow it to be. On a scale of 1-10, how does this feel?

4. For additional help, read Miller or The Women's Way Through the 12 Steps by Stephanie S. Covington.

How Your Values Affect Your Weight and Self-esteem

Values are those beliefs which you find uncompromising and which help to define who you are. When you think of your values, you generally think beyond the physical aspect of how you look. Underline those values that are important to you. Circle the values that you do not have, but would like.

Caring	Forgiving	Kind	Popular
Courageous	Generous	Lovable	Reliable
Dependable	Honest	Mature	Self-worthy
Enthusiastic	Hopeful	Opinionated	Tolerant
Faithful	Inquisitive	Patient	Trusting

Honesty and Its Effect on
Your Weight and Self-esteem

Most people with eating disorders are honest, hard-working, dependable people until it comes to food or their bodies. But they can be dishonest in ways they would not be in other area of their lives. They often will lie about what they eat and the amount of exercise they get.

Even though anorexics do have high values including honesty, they often lie because it is important to not get fat. They will say they had a huge lunch so they don't have to eat dinner when they haven't eaten anything all day. They see this as survival, not lying.

Many bulimics shoplift. Some shoplift to get food they can't afford to buy. Others shoplift when they are embarrassed about the large quantities of laxatives they use. Others say they started shoplifting food and got into bigger items because they never got caught and felt talented at it. A few get a thrill of outsmarting the store authority and the challenge of not getting caught. Others explain their shoplifting is the feeling of no matter how much food, clothes, jewelry, or material things they have, it is never enough. They keep trying to fill the emptiness inside. There are many bulimics, however, who do not shoplift and never would. Some bulimics feel the way they maintain their body weight is dishonest and has spread into being dishonest in other ways.

Binge eaters generally binge alone so they do not have to tell anyone about their binges. As a rule, males tend to be more up front. They may be embarrassed to eat large quantities in front of others, but if asked what they eat, they will be honest. It appears to be easier for males to be honest about their eating habits because society is more tolerant of their weight.

SELF-EVALUATION:

1. Ways in which I am dishonest:

    a. *I say I have eaten when I have not. (Anorexic)*
    b. *Maintaining my weight by purging. (Bulimic)*
    c. *I say I eat healthy when I mostly eat sweets and high fat foods. (Bulimic and Binge eater)*
    d. *I steal laxatives.*

2. My fears in being honest:

    a. *If I am honest that I have not eaten, my family will make me eat. (Anorexic)*
    b. *If I am honest about my purging, people will look at me with disgust. (Bulimic)*
    c. *If I say I have already eaten, I would not be able to eat again. (Binge eater)*

3. Beliefs I have in regard to honesty include:

    a. *I believe in it so strongly that I often tell too much.*
    b. *I have lied all my life. I don't know how to be honest.*
    c. *If I let others know the truth, they will hurt me.*

4. Beliefs that I could substitute for my present beliefs:

    a. *I can be honest without telling everything.*
    b. *Even though I have lied all my life, I don't have to continue to lie. The truth would help my self-esteem.*
    c. *I can be selective in how much to tell to whom in order to protect me from being hurt.*

5. How eating affects my honesty:

    a. *When I lie, I feel bad so I starve myself to punish myself. (Anorexic)*
    b. *When I am dishonest, I purge. (Bulimic)*
    c. *It is difficult for me to be honest with anyone about what I eat. (Binge eater)*

6. What action can I take to become more honest?

    a. *Each time I am honest, reward myself in ways other than with food.*
    b. *Tell a friend that I would like her to help me become more honest. Each time I lie to her I will tell her that I have lied.*
    c. *When I tell a lie, I write about it in my journal. In my journal indicate what I could say instead of a lie.*

EXERCISES:

1. Visualize yourself being honest. On a scale of 1-10, how do you feel when you are dishonest? When you are honest?

2. Journal your feelings and thoughts in regard to your honesty. (After the lie, write the truth several times until you get comfortable with the truth.)

3. For additional help, read Desperately Seeking Self by Viola Fodor or Where Are You Going? Guide to Spiritual Journey by Swami Muktananada.

Forgive Yourself and Others

To forgive someone means to pardon that person and give up your resentment. You will need to let go of your urge to punish. When you forgive those in your past that you have not forgiven, you feel less burdened and lighter in weight. You carry around extra baggage when you don't let go of past hurts. You forgive another person not for her benefit, but for yours. The decision to forgive someone else arises out of a desire to be at peace with you and others. When you forgive, you gain more from the experience than the person you forgave. It is an expression of self-worth because it lets you get on with your life in a healthy, productive way. You forgive for your serenity, peace of mind and ability to function with enthusiasm. Your anguish and sense of betrayal doesn't hurt the other person, but it could destroy you.

These are the reasons Overeaters Anonymous has you make amends to those you wish to forgive as an important part of their program. You don't just forgive and forget. By forgetting a major life betrayal or injury, you forget who you are and what has helped shape you.

SELF EVALUATION:

1. Persons in my life I need to forgive:

2. Ways I need to forgive myself:

    a. For not being perfect. (Anorexic)
    b. For purging.(Bulimic)
    c. For bingeing. (Binge eater)

3. My greatest fear in forgiving people and myself:

    a. They may hurt me again or get away with it.
       (What action can you take to make sure this doesn't happen?)

    b. If I forgive myself, I might make the same mistake again.
       (Sometimes we make the same mistake over and over before we are able to learn from it.)

    c. They may want to intrude in my life in a way I do not wish.
       (You are in charge of how involved you allow others to be in your life.)

4. When I don't forgive others or myself, it influences how I eat.

    a. When I do not forgive myself, I beat myself up and overeat.
    b. When I hold on to grudges, I have taken space and energy that could be used in a more productive way.
    c. When I don't forgive, I stuff the feeling with food.

EXERCISES:

1. Visualize yourself forgiving the person or persons you need to forgive. On a scale of 1-10, how does it feel not to be carrying this extra weight around?

2. Write in your journal a letter to the person or persons that you need to ask for their forgiveness. You may wish to send them your letter or you may want to ask for their forgiveness in person. It is also possible that writing about it is enough.

3. For additional help, read Learning to Forgive by Doris Donnelly or How to Forgive When You Don't Know How by Bishop and Grunte.

Develop Patience with Yourself and Others

You probably have little patience with yourself. You want to get to your ideal weight and you want it now. You are often much more patient with others than yourself. If you could treat yourself as kindly as you do others, you would feel better. You did not learn to eat the way you now eat or be the size you are overnight. Therefore, you are not going to change your weight overnight either. Take one day at a time or one hour at a time and you will feel less impatient. It is difficult to be patient when you lose weight and then hit a plateau in your weight loss. This happens to everyone. Be patient with yourself so that you lose weight that does not come back. Make lifetime changes, not quick fixes.

SELF EVALUATION:

1. **What are the areas of my life when I am the most impatient with myself?**

    a. *My weight and eating. I want to lose weight now.*
    b. *When others don't get their responsibilities done in time.*
    c. *When others don't do what I tell them.*
    d. *When I have not done my best.*

2. **What role models do I have that respond different from me?**
3. **What action can I take to become more patient?**

    a. *Set small realistic goals rather than such large unattainable goals.*
    b. *Be realistic about what changes I can make.*
    c. *Affirm and love myself.*
    d. *Change my negative thinking to affirming thoughts.*

4. **How is my eating related to my lack of patience?**

    a. *The more impatient I am, the more I starve myself. (Anorexic)*
    b. *The more impatient I am, the faster I eat. (Bulimic and binge eater)*
    c. *The more patient and loving I am with myself, the less I need to turn to food for love.*

177

EXERCISES:

1. Visualize yourself with a lot of patience toward yourself with regard to food and your body. What are you doing in this visualization that you can do in real life? On a scale of 1-10, how does that feel? What do you need to do to make this happen?

2. Write in your journal thoughts and feelings you have related to developing more patience. List the ways you are impatient. Next to each, write an action you can take to be more patient.

3. For additional help, read Patience Pays Off by James Sherman.

Trust and Its Effect on Your Weight and Self-esteem

You have to trust yourself before you can trust others. You may have good reasons not to trust others. If no adult was there for you as an infant when trust was first developed, it will be difficult to trust others. However, when you learn to trust yourself, you will then learn to trust others. It starts with you trusting you before able to trust others.

You are probably asking, how can you trust yourself when you have betrayed your body? This doesn't mean you have to continue to do so for the rest of your life. It is also important to give yourself some credit rather than to think how your body has betrayed you. What have you succeeded in? How have you not betrayed yourself? When do you trust yourself? Take these areas of success and use them in areas where you have failed. Rather than judge your failures, learn from them. You don't have to repeat the same mistakes. Regard your mistakes as opportunities to learn.

Anorexics, bulimics, and binge eaters find it difficult to trust themselves or others. Their history of failure with their weight makes it difficult for them to believe that they can trust themselves to stop this abuse of their bodies. Anorexics have trust in themselves as to when they have to eat in order not to pass out. Sometimes they miscalculate and end up in an emergency room. This may scare them enough to get help.

178

SELF EVALUATION:

1. When do I trust myself?

    a. When I write down what I eat.
    b. When I follow a food plan.
    c. When I make a promise to a friend.

2. When do I not trust myself?

    a. When I eat alone.
    b. When I eat out or go to a party.
    c. When I drink.

3. Beliefs I have in regard to trust:

    a. It is better not to trust than to be disappointed.
    (When you don't trust you miss out on life. Perhaps you need to be more selective of the people you trust.)

    b. Why should I trust myself when I have never done anything right?
    (Dwell on what you do well instead of your mistakes.)

    c. It feels so much safer to not trust. That way I don't get hurt.
    (Doesn't this make you feel isolated?)

EXERCISES:

1. Visualize trusting yourself and others. Take a situation where you distrust the most and imagine yourself reacting in a very different way than you usually do. What action do you need to take to have this happen?

2. Make a list of ways you do trust. Next, make a list of how you don't trust. After each item indicate what action you can take to build trust.

3. For additional help, read <u>Rebuilding Trust</u> by Schneider and Schneider or watch <u>Body Trust Video</u> by Production West.

How to Have Hope

People with eating problems lose hope. This feeling of hopelessness is often the result of their failure to find something that works for them. It is difficult to feel hopeful when nothing in the past has worked with your weight. When you feel hopeless, you feel nothing you do will work, so you stop trying because at least you won't fail again.

To change hopelessness to hope, you must change your thoughts and take action. When you don't do anything, you feel hopeless. It is important to change your thoughts from "I can't" to "I can and I will."

Anorexics, bulimics and binge eaters are often afraid to have hope because of their past failures. Often, their hope that things can be different is what they seek from therapy. Hope prompts action. We must be hopeful in order to feel alive.

SELF EVALUATION:

1. I feel hopeless about:

    a. My weight.
    b. Ever changing my obsessive thoughts about my weight and looks.
    c. Everything.
    d. Turning my life around.
    e. My looks.

2. What do I need to change in order to feel hopeful?

    a. My pessimistic thoughts.
    b. Change my thought that I can't do something to I know I can.
    c. Take a day at a time.

3. What has worked for me in the past that I could do now?

    a. I was hopeful when I had different friends.
    b. I could go back to church.
    c. Ask my higher power for help.
    d. Spend less time alone.
    e. Exercise.

4. What beliefs keep me from feeling hopeful?

    a. I have not succeeded in the past, therefore I can't succeed in the future.

    b. My family is fat, therefore I will be fat.

    c. I do not have what it takes to succeed.

    d. When I am hopeful, I get disappointed.

5. What beliefs could I have to make me feel hopeful?

    a. I am in control of what happens to me in the future no matter what has been true in the past. My past does not have to dictate my future.

    b. It is true I will have to work harder to overcome my eating problems when my family is obese, but it does not mean I can't change my habits.

    c. When I say I can't succeed, I probably keep myself from experiencing success.

6. Action I can take to become hopeful:

    a. Be realistic in what I attempt to achieve.

    b. Visualize what I want to have happen. Then go for it.

    c. Be like the engine who said, "I think I can. I think I can."

EXERCISES:

1. Visualize yourself feeling hopeful instead of hopeless. On a scale of 1-10, how does this feel? See yourself achieving what you want.

2. List the ways you feel hopeful and ways you feel hopeless. After the hopeless feelings, write what action you can take to feel hopeful.

3. Write about hope in your journal. Underline those thoughts that indicate hope and those that show hopelessness with different colored pens.

4. For additional help, read <u>Hope and Recovery</u> by Thayne and Markosian or <u>Images of Hope</u> by William Lynch.

Spiritual Evaluation

BEHAVIOR	USUAL PATTERN (1-10)	ACTION TO TAKE (1-10)
Higher Power	*Have lost faith in my higher power.* *(1)*	*Ask for help from my higher power as I need help.* *(8)*
Caring About Others	*I don't pay any attention to what others feel.* *(2)*	*Be nice to myself and to others* *(8)*
Faithful	*I have cheated on my partner.* *(2)*	*I can be faithful instead of having affairs.* *(8)*
Forgiveness	*Parents keep asking me to get help for my eating disorder, but I always refuse.* *(2)*	*Ask parents for forgiveness for the problems I have caused them.* *(9)*
Honesty	*I say I haven't purged when I have.* *(2)*	*Write what I feel prior to bingeing and purging.* *(9)*

BEHAVIOR	USUAL PATTERN (1-10)	ACTION TO TAKE (1-10)
Hope	*I feel there is no hope for my eating and weight problems.* *(1)*	*I can change my thinking to what I can do.* *(8)*
Trust	*I don't trust anyone.* *(2)*	*Start learning to trust by having a pet.* *(9)*
Patience	*I get so impatient and want this weight issue to be over now.* *(1)*	*It has taken me 20 years to develop this problem, so I guess I can give myself time to make changes slowly.* *(7)*
Courage	*I do not feel courageous at all.* *(2)*	*Take some risks.* *(8)*

CHAPTER SEVEN

Love Your Sexuality to Change Your Weight and Self-esteem

*Y*our sexual self is an important part of you. Loving your body is an important aspect of your sexuality. It is difficult to feel sexual when you hate your body. As you learn to love your body, you will love your sexuality more. If you were taught as a child that sex was dirty, you probably have a more difficult time with your sexual feelings than if you were taught that your sexuality was a beautiful part of you. If you talked openly in your family about your sexual feelings as a child, you will not feel ashamed as an adult.

Many people get confused about their sexual feelings. When parents tell their teenagers to wait until they get married to be sexual, parents forget to distinguish the teenagers' feelings from their actions. Even if you encourage your teenager to wait to become sexual, acknowledge the fact that her sexual feelings are natural feelings, to accept as normal.

I recall an obese client who was aware that her fat protected her from sexual feelings. She knew she would be unfaithful and promiscuous if she lost weight. She felt while she was morbid-obese and dependent on her husband, she could not leave the marriage. When she became more independent, she decided that she no longer wanted to stay in the marriage. As she lost weight, she dressed more colorfully and provocatively. She did act on her sexual feelings and often made unwise decisions until she realized this was not healthy for her. She went from hiding her sexual feelings to acting them out before she was able to reach a middle ground.

■■■

Anorexics often want to deny their sexual feelings. Some bulimics are promiscuous and have sex to try to fill their feelings of emptiness. Sometimes bulimics have several sexual partners in order for them to feel accepted by others. Binge eaters sometimes overeat because they are not comfortable with their sexuality. They feel if they get fat enough, abusers or partners will not bother them for sex.

Men tend to view their sexuality in a different way than women. Men find lovemaking helps them to feel more intimate. Women want intimacy prior to making love. Thus, men must try to be intimate and loving outside the bedroom. Males tend to be more comfortable with their genitals because they and others view themselves in men's public rest rooms.

SELF EVALUATION:

1. **The relationship of my sexual feelings in regard to my body, weight, and food:**

     a. When I deny my sexual feelings, I stuff the feelings with food.
     b. My sexual feelings are uncomfortable for me to accept.
     c. I fear my sexual feelings because of prior abuse.
     d. I use my fat to hide my sexual feelings for fear that if I become thin, I will become promiscuous.
     e. I feel that I am different from others because I have never discussed my sexual feelings with others. Therefore I never had the chance to find out my feelings are normal.
     f. I feel all sexuality is abuse because of my past sexual abuse.

2. **What were you taught in regard to your sexuality?**

     a. I am not comfortable with my sexuality because it was not a subject openly discussed in our home.
     b. I was taught that if I allowed my sexual feelings to be present I would lose control and become a slut.
     c. I was taught my sexuality was something to be shamed of rather than a beautiful part of myself.
     d. I was taught that my sexuality was beautiful and natural and to not abuse my body.
     e. My sexuality was sacred.

3. **I wish to change my thoughts toward my sexuality with respect to:**

   a. *Sex is not dirty or bad. It is a natural feeling and a way to express love.*
   b. *I like to think my comfort with my sexuality does not have to mean I will become promiscuous.*
   c. *I want to love my sexuality and my body rather than fear it.*

4. **Fears I have in regard to my sexuality:**

   a. *I am afraid to enjoy my sexuality for fear I will get hurt.*
   b. *I fear I will act like a slut.*
   c. *If I get in touch with my sexuality, I will not think about anything else.*
   d. *I am afraid I will contact AIDS like my friend if I become sexual again.*

5. **Action I can take to help me become comfortable with my sexuality:**

   a. *Talk to my lover about my discomfort with my sexuality.*
   b. *Be honest with my lover about what I like and dislike about our sexual habits.*
   c. *Talk to my friends about sex to see if my feelings are like their feelings.*

6. **What and how much I eat is related to my sexual energy and freedom:**

   a. *I starve myself to avoid my sexuality because it is safer. (Anorexic)*
   b. *I purge to rid me of my sexual feelings. (Bulimic)*
   c. *I binge to protect myself from getting hurt. (Binge eater)*

EXERCISES:

1. Visualize yourself being comfortable with your sexuality. On a scale of 1-10, how does that feel?

2. Write in your journal your feelings and thoughts about your sexuality. Write about what parts of your sexuality you want to become more comfortable. What action do you need to take to get there?

3. For additional help, read Human Sexual Responses by Masters and Johnson or Joy of Sex by Alex Comfort.

Overcome the Trauma of Sexual Abuse

When sexual abuse occurs to a child, she has the feeling that she caused the abuse and it was her fault. This results in shame. No matter what you did as a child, you did not deserve the abuse. If abuse occurs and you haven't told anyone, you will get a sense of relief when you share it with someone you trust. Secrets are similar to denying feelings. The more we work to deny our abuse, the greater the impact on our lives. We don't have to let our abuse ruin our lives. Oprah is a great example of a star who didn't allow her abuse to keep her from a successful life. It doesn't have to interfere with your life either.

I feared going to the doctor because I was afraid he would find out I had been sexually abused. My abuser told me if I told anyone he would hurt my parents. I remember the first time I told someone I had been sexually abused as a child. I was a sophomore in college. I remember my friend saying, "Sharon, you have done nothing wrong." I was shocked to hear this reaction, as I was sure I had done something awful. What a relief!

My abuse caused me so much shame that I worked harder to show I was a good person. I believe my abuse and its affect motivated me to become a therapist. I wanted to help others who experienced the same trauma.

Sometimes the anorexic tries to compensate for the sexual abuse by being a "good girl" and not wanting to disappoint anyone. It appears fewer anorexics have experienced sexual abuse than bulimics or binge eaters. Many bulimics describe how they purge to cleanse themselves of the horrible abuse they experienced.

Females with eating disorders are more likely than males to have a history of sexual abuse. However, we are now seeing more male patients with an abusive history. When more males come forward with their eating problems, we may see more of a correlation with sexual abuse. Below are some possible indicators if an adult has had sexual abuse as a child. These symptoms don't necessarily mean sexual abuse has occurred. The symptoms could be a result of numerous causes.

Symptoms of Sexual Abuse

a. Feelings absent during sex: Out-of-body experience.
b. Anger or fear of the opposite sex.
c. Seductive behavior which seems inappropriate.
d. Promiscuous behavior.
e. Intense reaction to genital examination.
f. Aversion to sex.
g. Sexual identity confusion.
h. Dreams of sexual assault.

SELF EVALUATION:

1. I was sexually abused by:

    a. My father.
    b. My baby sitter.
    c. My uncle.

2. Why I'm afraid to talk about my abuse:

    a. It will make me feel worse to talk about it.
    (That depends on what affect it has in your present life. If your silence interferes with your sexual enjoyment, you may feel better when you bring it out in the open and talk about it.)

    b. It will bring up all the old feelings I have buried.
    (If you have truly buried these feelings, you don't have to bring them up.)

    c. It will feel as if I was being abused again.
    (It is not as difficult to talk about it as it was to be abused.)

3. **My beliefs related to my sexual abuse:**

   a. *If I had been a better person, this would not have happened.*
   (This had nothing to do with what you did. It is a statement about the sickness of the adult, not you as the child.)

   b. *I caused my abuse.*
   (You as a child did nothing to cause your abuse, no matter what the adult told you.)

   c. *If I tell, the abuser will hurt someone I love.*
   (Abusers do tell children that they will hurt someone the child loves, if they tell. This keeps the child quiet and scared. Contact authorities for protection.)

4. **Beliefs I could use to help me overcome my sexual abuse:**

   a. *The child within needs my love and support, not blame.*
   b. *How sad it was my child within was taken advantage of by a sick adult who did this to me.*
   c. *I deserve to have a healthy adult sex life no matter what was done to me as a child.*

5. **My eating is related to my abuse by:**

   a. *I don't eat to make myself so skinny that people will feel sorry for me and not abuse me again. (Anorexic)*
   b. *I am so used to having my body abused that I continue to abuse it by purging. (Bulimic)*
   c. *I overeat to make myself unattractive, so I won't be sexually abused again.(Binge eater)*

EXERCISES:

1. Write a letter to your abuser telling him how you feel. You don't need to send the letter for it to be helpful to you. If you wish to confront your abuser, practice saying what you want to say. It may be helpful to practice with a friend first.

2. Visualize yourself letting go of the sexual abuse that was done to you as a child. You no longer give the abuser any power and you are free of the past. Give this to your higher power and be free. On a scale of 1-10, how does this feel?

3. For additional help, read <u>Sexual Abuse and Eating Disorders</u> by Schwartz and Cohn or <u>Guide for Survivors of Sexual Abuse</u> by Wendi Maltz.

Victimization No More

If you were victimized as a child, there was probably little you could have done to protect yourself. It is important to realize that as an adult you no longer need to be a victim. The victim role is one in which you say, "Poor me" and feel helpless and powerless. If you play the victim role, the abuser will know how to find you. You don't have to continue to be the victim even if it is all you have ever known. Take charge of your life to avoid becoming a victim. Make your own decisions rather than allowing others to make your decisions for you. WHEN YOU FEEL LIKE A VICTIM, TAKE ACTION. You can feel like a victim when you don't act to resolve your issues. Your weight can make you feel like a victim when you don't act to change it.

Anorexics rarely take a victim's role because they are not likely to let anyone else make their decisions. Bulimics and binge eaters are frequently victims and often feel that they have no choice. Since men are less used to a subordinate role, they tend to feel less victimized than females.

SELF EVALUATION:

1. **I was victimized as a child when:**
2. **When are the times I feel like a victim as an adult?**
3. **Beliefs I could change to no longer feel like a victim:**

    a. *What I think, need, and feel are more important than what others think of me.*
    b. *I am entitled to stand up for myself and protect myself.*
    c. *I don't have to do what others tell me to do.*

191

4. **Why I am afraid to give up my victim role:**

   a. *I have played this role all my life. It is all I know.*
   b. *Negative attention is better than no attention at all.*
   c. *I am afraid that no one will like me if I change.*
      (They might like you more.)

5. **Action I could take to get out of the victim role:**

   a. *Think in terms of what I can do instead of what I can't do.*
   b. *I am not going to let anyone take advantage of me anymore.*
   c. *Ask myself what I can do instead of asking for help.*
      (When we are in charge of our actions, we are no longer
      the victim.)

EXERCISES:

1. Visualize yourself out of the victim role. You are no longer
   powerless, but powerful. You respond to your needs instead of
   pleasing others. On a scale of 1-10, how does it feel to be a victim?
   No longer a victim?

2. In your journal, write other thoughts and feelings you have about
   victimization. List ways you feel like a victim. Indicate what action
   you can take to no longer be one.

3. For additional help, read Body Betrayed: A Deeper Understanding of
   Women, Eating Disorders and Treatment by Kathryn Zerbe or
   Courage to Heal Workbook: For Men and Woman Survivors of
   Sexual Abuse by Laura Davis.

Value Your Male and Female Traits

It is important for each of us to recognize that we have both male and
female traits. Traits society considers as male characteristics that we want
to incorporate into our personalities include strength, dominance,
assertiveness, and energy. Female characteristics we want to include are
sensitivity, caring, loving, and nurturing. It is the hope that as society

changes, it will encourage all to exhibit both sets of qualities rather than to stereotype them to a particular sex. Too often males deny their femininity for fear they won't be masculine enough. Females often deny their strengths for fear they won't be feminine enough. A healthy person allows both to be present and feels comfortable with each.

Anorexics often starve themselves to have man-like bodies to please their fathers who wanted a son. They may also be trying to rid themselves of their menstruation and femininity. Bulimic and binge eaters may have a difficult time getting in touch with their male traits. It is important for them to get approval from all, so they ignore their needs. They may appear to lack assertiveness and leadership.

There appears to be a high relationship between males with eating disorders and the gay population. Gay men tend to be more concerned about their bodies and appearance than the general male population, therefore, more gays have eating disorders. Lesbians, however, tend to be more tolerant of any body shape and have fewer eating disorders.

SELF EVALUATION:

1. **Male traits I value in myself include:**
2. **Female traits I value in myself include:**
3. **Beliefs I could use to develop both my maleness and femaleness:**

> **a. Females:** *Just because I develop my male traits doesn't mean I can't be feminine.*
>
> **b. Males:** *When I get in touch with my female traits, I am more sensitive and nurturing, which makes me more attractive to my partner.*

4. **My masculine and feminine traits influence my eating by:**

> a. *I don't eat so I can look like a male. (Female anorexic)*
> b. *When I deny my feminine or masculine traits, I binge. (Bulimic and binge eater)*
> c. *I overeat to be less feminine so that I am not sexually abused.*
> d. *I hate myself when I am not assertive as I could be. I punish myself for being so gutless by starving myself or overeating.*

EXERCISES:

1. Visualize yourself developing your feminine and masculine traits. How do you see yourself differently than you are now? What feelings does this bring up for you?

2. Write about your feminine and masculine traits. What do you need to do to have a balance with these traits?

3. For additional help, read <u>Men Are From Mars and Women Are From Venus</u> by John Gray or <u>Males with Eating Disorders</u> by Arnold E. Anderson.

Sexual Evaluation

BEHAVIOR	USUAL PATTERN (1-10)	ACTION TO TAKE (1-10)
Sexuality	*I am ashamed of my sexual feelings and I try to deny the sexual part of my being.* *(2)*	*Tell myself my sexual feelings are normal, natural, and beautiful.* *(9)*
Sexual Abuse	*Fear of being abused again.* *(1)*	*Take karate lessons so I can feel safer and not have to live in fear of not being able to protect myself.* *(9)*

BEHAVIOR	USUAL PATTERN (1-10)	ACTION TO TAKE (1-10)
Victim No More	*I was a victim as a child.* *(1)*	*As an adult I will never let anyone take advantage of me again. I am no longer helpless like when I was a child.* *(9)*
Female/ Male Traits	*I deny my masculine traits for fear I won't be feminine.* *(2)*	*Allow myself to feel both my masculine and feminine parts to feel more whole.* *(9)*

CHAPTER EIGHT

Assertive Skills to Change Your Weight and Self-esteem

*I*f you are able to be assertive, to stand up for your rights, can say no and don't allow others to walk all over you, you will feel good about yourself. When you are not assertive and allow others to take advantage of you, the anger you feel toward the person who hurt you is turned inward. This can cause you to turn to food to make you feel better. When you use food this way, it is a temporary fix--a high from enjoying the food and then a low for having eaten it when you didn't need it.

An anorexic tries to make herself feel invisible by not eating. If she's invisible, she doesn't have to confront others. She acts as if she's not present, allowing her to not have to deal with her problems. When another person tries to control her or tell her what to eat, however, the tiger in her comes out and she promptly tells others they aren't going to tell her how to eat. Sometimes the control she has over her eating is the only control she has. It's not uncommon for bulimics to purge or binge eaters to overeat after they've let someone walk over them. Their anger is turned inward. It is rewarding to hear someone learn to defend herself and say, "I told her exactly what I thought and I didn't have to binge afterwards. It felt wonderful."

▰▰▰

How to Be Assertive
Rather Than Aggressive or Passive

Sometimes people are confused about the difference between assertive, aggressive, and passive behaviors. Passive behavior is when you allow others to make choices for you. You do nothing. When you are passive, you express your needs indirectly to avoid conflicts. You feel helpless, find it difficult to say "no" and don't know how to meet your needs.

Aggressive behavior is when you act at the expense of another usually by depreciating them. You achieve your goals at the expense of others. This behavior results in conflict and a desire for control. You are pushy and overbearing.

Assertive behavior is when you love yourself, feel good about yourself, and express your needs directly, but not at the expense of others. You achieve your goals. This behavior results in reduced anger and the ability to stand up for your rights.

Anorexics tend to be able to stand up for what they want when it is related to their eating and weight. But they may be passive when it relates to non-food or weight issues. They tend to deny what they feel and are unable to express to others what they feel. They often pretend to be the perfect person. They don't want anyone to know the conflict they feel inside.

Bulimic and binge eaters are often passive when anyone makes a comment about their weight. They are so sensitive about their weight they are at a loss as to what to say. They may be assertive in other areas of their lives. Some tend to be aggressive when they try to assert themselves. We all learn to be aggressive before we become assertive. It takes practice. Remember you have the right to make mistakes, but you want to learn from your mistakes.

Beliefs that interfere with the ability to be assertive:
1. It is shameful to make mistakes.
2. It is selfish to put one's own needs first.
3. Others will think I am stupid.
4. Others will get mad at me.

| 5. Keep my ideas to myself that differ from authority. |
| 6. Others have the right to know all about me. |
| 7. It is improper to question others' actions. |
| 8. Others' thoughts are more important than my own. |
| 9. Always be consistent and logical. |
| 10. I can't ask others for things that may inconvenience them. |
| 11. I don't have the right to refuse requests from others. |
| 12. I am not as smart as others are. |
| 13. Others will think I am too forceful. |
| 14. Others are not interested in what I think. |
| 15. I don't have the right to be angry with others. |

Beliefs that help me to be assertive:
1. It is my right to put myself first as long as it does not hurt others.
2. I have the right to make mistakes.
3. It is my right to judge my behavior but not be judgmental.
4. It is O.K. to say I don't know or understand.
5. I give myself permission to say I don't care.
6. It is my right to have my own opinions and convictions.
7. It is my right to change my mind.
8. I protest unfair treatment or criticism.
9. I don't need to offer an excuse.
10. It is my right to ask others for help.
11. It is O.K. to refuse requests.
12. It is my right to love myself.

Examples of passive, aggressive, and assertive behaviors

a. You have made a new goal to eat healthily. You have been invited to go to a friend's home for dinner. This is an old friend with whom you used to binge. You know she will expect you to have another binge with her. You say:

1. *If you want me to come, I will.*
   (This is a passive comment because you want to please the other person rather than express your new eating style.)

2. *No way. I'm not going to set myself up and eat all that food and binge like you. I don't do that anymore. If you had any guts, which I know you don't, you'd stop bingeing too.*
   (This is aggressive because you have hurt the other person and have put her down.)

3. *I would love to spend time with you, however, it is important to let you know I have promised myself not to binge anymore.*
   (This is an assertive comment because you have stated your need without hurting the other person.)

b. A fellow co-worker wants to know if she can borrow some money to eat out. She has not paid you back the five dollars she borrowed last time you went out. You say to her:

1. *O.K.*
   (This is a passive comment because you have avoided the issue of the money she owes you.)

2. *Find some other sucker. You are not going to get any more money from me since you are irresponsible.*
   (This is an aggressive comment because you have made a derogatory comment about the other person without stating clearly your needs.)

3. *I wouldn't mind loaning you money for lunch on the condition that you pay me back tomorrow. I also would like the five dollars you owe me from the last time we went out.*
   (An assertive statement because you have stated your needs without degrading her.)

Aggressive Evaluation

COMMENTS	AGGRESSIVE RESPONSES (1-10)	ASSERTIVE RESPONSES (1-10)
How awful dieting is.	*You don't want to look like that forever, do you?* (2)	*Yes, isn't dieting awful? That is why I don't diet any longer.* (9)
You'd rather be fat than thin?	*I'd rather be me than you.* (3)	*I like every ounce of my body.* (8)
Any comment not spoken directly to you, but clearly intended for you to hear.	*Drop dead.* (3)	*I'm fat, but I am not deaf.* (9)
You've gained weight.	*So what? Get off your high horse to try to make yourself be better than everyone else.* (3)	*How nice of you to notice.* (9)
You are fat. You need to start jogging.	*You're rude. Wash your mouth with soap.* (4)	*I prefer swimming.* (8)

BEHAVIOR	USUAL PATTERN (1-10)	ACTION TO TAKE (1-10)
You have such a nice personality. It is a shame you are so fat.	*Why would I want my body to match your narrow mind?* *(5)*	*Thank you. It goes along with my beautiful body.* *(9)*
You'd be such a pretty girl, if you would lose weight.	*You would be such a smart person if you didn't make such a dumb comment.* *(4)*	*I am beautiful just as I am. I'm pretty now.* *(9)*
You shouldn't be eating that dessert.	*What makes you think its any of your business what I eat?* *(4)*	*You are right. I don't need it. I want it.* *(9)*
I'd date you if you lost some weight.	*Well, I wouldn't date anyone like you, even if you had a brain.* *(2)*	*If you don't like me fat, what makes you think you would like me thin?* *(9)*
Are you pregnant?	*What a stupid question, you idiot.* *(1)*	*No, but the night is still young.* *(8)*

SELF EVALUATION:

1. Ways I am passive:

    a. I don't speak up for my needs.
    b. I let others walk all over me.
    c. I don't let others know what I am feeling, thinking, or believing.
    d. I am quiet when I have something important to contribute.

2. Ways I am aggressive:

    a. I put others down.
    b. I step on others in order to get what I want.
    c. I am insensitive to others' feelings.
    d. I hurt others by my statements.

3. Ways I am assertive:

    a. I say how I feel.
    b. I tell how the problem affects me.
    c. I let others know what I think in a gentle way.

EXERCISES:

1. Take a situation in which you were passive. Visualize yourself being assertive in that situation. What would you have said? Practice saying it until you can feel comfortable when you say it in the next situation.

2. Take a situation in which you were aggressive. Visualize yourself being assertive in that situation. What would you say? On a scale of 1-10, how does it feel to be aggressive? Assertive?

3. For additional help, read Creative Aggression. Art of Assertive Living by George Bach and Herb Goldberg.

Assertiveness to Enhance Your Self-esteem

Most people find it difficult to express their needs in some areas more than in others. Below are some of the more difficult areas for people to assert themselves. After each type, indicate when, with whom, and why this type is difficult for you.

SELF EVALUATION:

1. It's difficult for me to give compliments when:

> a. *I am afraid I will seem phony.*
> b. *I am afraid of the other person's response.*
> c. *I am with someone in authority.*
> d. *I am wrapped up in my own problems.*

2. It's difficult for me to receive a compliment because:

> a. *I am not used to getting any.*
> b. *I am embarrassed because I don't see myself positively.*
> c. *I don't know how to respond.*
> d. *I don't like attention drawn to me.*

3. It is difficult for me to express personal opinions because:

> a. *I am afraid I will sound silly.*
> b. *I don't believe my thoughts are as important as others.*
> c. *I don't think about my opinions. I am busy trying to figure out what I think others want to hear.*

4. It is difficult for me to express negative feelings, especially anger because:

> a. *I am afraid others won't like me.*
> b. *I am afraid I will be out of control.*
> c. *I was taught that if I don't have anything nice to say, keep my mouth shut.*

5. It is difficult for me to refuse requests because:

    a. I am afraid others won't like me.
    b. I want to make them happy and I am afraid they will get mad.
    c. I don't know how to say no.

6. Fears I have of becoming assertive:

    a. I will become aggressive instead of assertive.
    b. I will become like my obnoxious uncle.
    c. When I deal with people in a new way, I mess up.
    (As you practice your assertive skills, you will get better.)

7. I tie my lack of assertiveness to my eating disorder by:

    a. When I let others walk all over me, I get so mad at myself I starve myself. (Anorexic)
    b. When I don't speak up for my rights, I get angry with myself. I then stuff the feeling by bingeing. (Bulimic and binge eater)
    c. When I don't confront others, I eat to make me feel better.

EXERCISES:

1. Visualize yourself being assertive at times when it is difficult for you. Practice what you would do and say, then do it. Start with being assertive with people you don't know and do not care what they think, such as people in a grocery line. When you are successful in one area, then visualize yourself in another situation.

2. Write about a time when you were aggressive. Then write what you could have done differently to be assertive.

3. Go through your journal and mark the times you were assertive, passive, and aggressive with different colored markers. It will help you to be aware and it is a way to chart your progress.

4. For additional help with assertiveness, take an assertiveness training class or read <u>Your Assertive Right</u> by Alberti & Emmons or <u>The New Assertive Woman</u> by Bloom, Coburn, and Pearlman.

Avoid Manipulating or Being Manipulated

No one can manipulate you without your permission. When you are angry with others who manipulate you, ask yourself what you do to allow others to act this way. Only you are in charge of whether or not you allow someone to manipulate you or whether they can make you do something against your will. You are assertive when you don't allow someone to manipulate you.

Manipulators find those who are willing to be manipulated. They know how to say things people want to hear. Manipulators quickly recognize weaknesses in others and use that person's vulnerability to their advantage. Manipulators are people whose self-esteem is based on what others do for them. They don't think in terms of how to meet their own needs, but rather how they can get others to meet their needs instead. Manipulators are intelligent, witty and charming in demeanor and people are drawn to them. It is difficult to see that their sensitivity is not genuine. They pretend to be your friend to get what they want. They are often isolated or lonely because others get tired of their tactics and want little to do with them.

Anorexics are often great manipulators. Parents often will allow the anorexic to rule the house. The anorexic gets to decide where the family will go for dinner because if it is not where she wants to go, she will either not go or not eat. Other children get very tired and angry at how the anorexic's needs seem to have priority.

Bulimics and binge eaters are not generally manipulators but are manipulated. Others learn that bulimics and binge eaters are great targets to be manipulated because they will try to please others rather than stand up for their rights.

SELF EVALUATION:

1. Ways I manipulate others:

    a. I let others think I am looking out for them when I am really looking out for me.
    b. I tell my family I won't go out to eat with them unless they go where I want.
    c. I buy others things in order for them to do what I want.

2. Ways I am manipulated:

    a. I let others walk all over me.
    b. I don't speak up for my rights.
    c. I do what others want in order for them to like me.

3. Beliefs that I have that contribute to my manipulation of others:

    a. It is my job to take care of myself. If others will let me take advantage of them, that is their problem.
    (This type of thinking will not work to your advantage.)

    b. When I love myself I see that my needs are met even if it means I manipulate others to achieve my goal.
    (People who love themselves do not exploit others.)

4. Beliefs I have that contribute to my being manipulated:

    a. It is important to keep the peace, so I do what others say.
    b. I am such a caretaker for others that I forget to take care of myself.
    c. I am afraid if I stand up to the person who manipulates me, he will get mad and not like me.
    (You do not need approval of persons who mistreat you.)

5. How being manipulated (or my manipulating) affects my eating:

    a. When I allow others to manipulate me, I feel bad so I eat to make myself feel better.
    b. When others allow me to manipulate them, it makes me lose respect for them for allowing the manipulation.

1. Visualize yourself not being manipulated or not manipulating. What would you do differently? Practice it over and over again until it becomes second nature to you.

2. Write in your journal about being manipulated or manipulating others. Underline with different colored pen examples when you manipulate others and are manipulated.

3. For additional help read <u>Manipulators</u> by Ben Bursten.

Say No

When you learn to say no to family, friends, and associates, it is similar to saying no to food. Until you can assert yourself, you will probably have a difficult time saying no to food. When you are able to say no, you will feel so good you won't need to turn to food for comfort. It may be easier to say no to others than it is to say no to food. No to food doesn't mean you don't eat, it only means you eat when you are physically hungry and not for emotional needs.

Most anorexics tend to have an easier time saying no to others than do bulimics or binge eaters. Most anorexics are so set on eating the way they want to eat that they don't allow others to interfere.

Bulimics and binge eaters generally find it difficult to say no because they want people to like them. Sometimes the obese binge eater will not say no because she feels she needs to please to compensate for her weight.

SELF EVALUATION:

1. When are the times it is difficult to say no?

    a. To my parents.
    b. To authority.
    c. When I feel insecure.
    d. When I am afraid of being abandoned.

2. When is it easy to say no?

    a. To people soliciting over the phone.
    b. To people I don't know.
    c. To my children.
    d. When I don't like the person and I don't care what
       they think.
    e. When I don't want to do what is asked of me.
    f. When I feel I couldn't do a good job.

3. Beliefs I could have to say no:

    a. It is important to be able to say no because I can't always
       do what others want me to do.
    b. I don't need to explain my reasons for saying no.
    c. Ask myself what would happen if no one said no. What
       makes it wrong for me to say no when others can?

EXERCISES:

1. Start to say no with a person you are most comfortable with and who you believe would accept your no. Then go to another person and another. It is also easier to start with strangers when you don't care what they think.

2. Visualize yourself saying no when it has been difficult in the past. When was it hard to say no? What could you have said? Practice this over and over in your mind until you are ready to do it. You will like how it feels.

3. Journal other thoughts and feelings you have regarding learning to say no. Keep a record of times when you would like to say no. Write no until you feel confident to say it.

4. For additional help, read <u>When I Say No, I Feel Guilty</u> by Manuel Smith.

Send "I" Messages

In order to assert yourself, you must know what you are feeling and you need to express that to another. You send an "I" message when you tell the other person what you feel about the situation and the effect it has on you. A "you" message is when you blame the other person for how you feel. When someone upsets you, ask yourself why it bothers you so much. It may give you clues as to what you don't like about yourself.

When you send an "I" message, you feel good about yourself. You then do not need to turn to food to feel better. When you send a "you" message, you feel guilty. An example of an "I" message is, *"I feel angry about the dishes being left on the table instead of in the sink. It makes more work for me."* A "you" message is *"You idiot, how many times do I have to tell you to put your dishes in the sink?"* Which would you respond to? How do you feel about yourself when you send the "I" message versus the "you" message? It is helpful to send "I" messages to your children, your spouse, your co-workers, friends and even to strangers.

SELF EVALUATION:

1. When do you say "I" messages?

    a. When I tell how I feel about the situation and the effect it has on me.
    b. When I am calm and rational.
    c. When I feel secure and confident.
    d. When I think before I speak.
    e. When I am not angry.

2. When do you say "you" messages?

    a. When I am mad.
    b. When I want to hurt the other person.
    c. When I talk before I think.
    d. When I am out of control.
    e. When I want to blame someone else rather than take responsibility for my own actions.

Send "I" Messages

"YOU" MESSAGES	"I" MESSAGES
You are so fat.	*I am concerned about how you seem to not care about yourself anymore.*
You are an idiot.	*I am sorry you have made the decision to quit school.*
You are always making mistakes.	*I am disappointed you continue to make errors in your reports because I have to correct them during my free time.*
Your starving is a sign of immaturity.	*I am concerned that starving will cause you medical problems.*
Your purging is disgusting.	*It scares me when you purge. I hate to see you hurt yourself.*
Are you ever going to stop bingeing?	*Is there anything I can do to be of help to you with your bingeing? It makes me sad to see you struggle.*
Your eating habits are horrible.	*It makes me sad to see how hard you struggle with your eating.*

"YOU" MESSAGES	"I" MESSAGES
Stop complaining.	*I get tired of hearing only complaints from you because it wears me down. Would you like for me to help you with this problem? It once was a problem for me too.*
You have no self-control. Look at all you eat.	*It makes me angry that all the food is gone, and there is not enough food for the rest of us.*
You are so selfish. All you ever think about is yourself.	*It makes me angry that you don't ask if I want a drink when you get up and get a drink for yourself.*
You are a slob.	*It would make me happy when the clothes in your room are picked up.*
You look terrible with all the weight you have gained.	*I am concerned about your health with the extra weight you have recently gained. You don't seem very happy lately. Is there anything you want to talk about?*
You are too skinny.	*I am afraid that you'll die and that would make me very sad. I would miss you.*

EXERCISES:

1. Think about the last time you sent a "you" message. What was the message? How could you send it as an "I" message instead? Use the chart above to help you learn to change your "you" messages to "I" messages.

2. Write in your journal thoughts and feelings in regard to sending "I" messages. Practice writing them until they are second nature to you.

3. For additional help, read <u>Parent Effectiveness Training</u> by Thomas Gordon.

How to Maintain Your Power

People who feel empowered generally like themselves. They feel in charge of their lives. They have respect for themselves, don't give their power to others, and don't feel victimized. The people who give their power to others feel victimized, helpless, or sorry for themselves. They also give power to food. Once a person learns to maintain her power with others, she usually finds it easier to maintain her power with food.

Anorexics usually feel empowered. They don't let anyone tell them what to do. Thus, they don't give their power to others, especially when it concerns food. When they don't eat, they let their starvation be in control.

Bulimics and binge eaters often turn to food because they let others walk all over them. Males with eating disorders feel they have little power because they feel they are too fat or too small. Males, however, tend to feel more empowered than females because females are often trained to be subordinate.

SELF EVALUATION:

1. Times I feel most empowered are:

    a. When I have said what I believe.
    b. When I take action for what I want.
    c. When I feel confident.

2. Times I give my power away are:

    a. When I am around authority figures.
    b. With food.
    c. When I am unsure of myself.

3. Beliefs I could have to become more empowered:

    a. I have the right to stand up to authority and anyone else who tries to take advantage of me.
    b. I won't become obnoxious just because I empower myself. In fact, I will get more respect from others, not less.
    c. People who are empowered don't need to be overbearing or unpleasant.

4. My relationship with food is related to my empowerment:

    a. When I give my power away, I stuff myself with food because I am disappointed with myself.
    b. When I feel empowered, I don't feel the need to overeat.
    c. My lack of power makes me feel less of myself, which makes me want to fill this emptiness with food.

EXERCISES:

1. Take an assertive class.

2. Take a situation in which you felt you had no power. Visualize yourself empowered in the same situation. Visualize what you say, feel, and hear. Practice doing it. Repeat this with a different situation.

3. Write in your journal other feelings and thoughts you have about empowerment. Write what action you can take to feel more powerful.

4. For additional help, read <u>Accepting Powerlessness Over Food Obsession</u> by Judy Hollis.

Assertive Evaluation

SITUATION	USUAL PATTERN (1-10)	ACTION TO TAKE (1-10)
Giving Compliments	*I give compliments all the time whether I mean it or not. I do this in hopes that others will like me.* (3)	*Give compliments only when I mean it so I will be sincere, which will help others to like me.* (8)
Receive Compliments	*I don't accept them because I just think they are trying to make me feel better.* (3)	*Say thank you and accept it. Try to internalize the compliments so I can start to believe them.* (9)
Express Personal Opinions	*I rarely express my opinions for fear of being ridiculed.* (1)	*Start by expressing an opinion I feel very strongly about.* (9)
Manipulation	*I am manipulating others to get what I want.* (2)	*I can be more flexible in not having to have things my way.* (7)
Refuse requests	*I am afraid I will have to owe them something.* (2)	*I am in charge of which requests I want to honor and refuse.* (8)

SITUATION	USUAL PATTERN (1-10)	ACTION TO TAKE (1-10)
Sending "I" Messages"	*I usually send "you" messages.* *(2)*	*I will try to say how I feel about the situation and the effect it has on me.* *(9)*
Sending "You" Messages	*I blame others.* *(2)*	*I can send messages of how I feel instead of blaming others.* *(9)*
Empower Myself	*I do not know how to empower myself.* *(1)*	*I am a good person and that makes me powerful.* *(9)*
Express Negative Feelings	*I deny all negative feelings.* *(2)*	*There are no negative feelings.* *(8)*
Say no	*I rarely say no because I want people to like me.* *(2)*	*Start by saying no to strangers.* *(8)*

C H A P T E R   N I N E

Reduce Stress to Change Your Weight and Self-esteem

*W*hen you are stressed, you probably eat too fast and too much. You use food to relieve the stress. You may not be able to give up your bingeing or purging until you learn other ways to deal with your stress.

Anorexics are extremely stressed. They work as hard at fasting as the workaholic who gets stressed at work because there is no other relief. If you dwell on any issue all day long, whether it is your weight or job, you get stressed. That is one reason anorexics exercise to excess. They get stressed out because they need to have constant control over their weight. Exercise releases this stress until they become so anorexic that they can't exercise any longer. They may not have enough strength to get out of bed.

Bulimics use purging as a means of tension release. In fact, many find it impossible to give up purging until they find other means to release their stress. When bulimics learn to relax and meditate, many find they can give up purging.

Binge eaters use food to help them relax temporarily. When they binge, they numb themselves from the stress and pressures of the day. This is why many find it difficult to control their eating in the evenings. When they learn to relax, they don't have the same need for food.

■■■

Before you can learn to relax and meditate, you need to get in touch with your body. If you disassociate from your body or ignore its signals, you don't know when you are stressed. It is important for you to learn your body's signals of when it is stressed, just like when your body is hungry. Once you recognize the early signals of stress in your body, you can respond by relaxing rather than eating.

Signs of Stress

1. Cold hands, especially if one hand is colder than the other.
2. Shortness of breath.
3. Becoming suddenly accident-prone.
4. Headaches.
5. Tiredness.
6. Sleeping too much or too little.
7. Indigestion.
8. Diarrhea.
9 Frequent urination.
10. Susceptibility to colds or virus.
11. Muscle spasms.
12. Tightness in jaw, back of the neck, shoulders, or lower back.
13. Inability to relax, concentrate, or focus.

When you recognize these signals, stop what you are doing, take several deep breaths, and try to relax. If tension shows itself through tapping toes or drumming fingers, take a quick brisk walk, do few jumping jacks or knee bends to relieve some of the tension.

The most important thing to defuse the stress or tension is to become conscious of your inner voice and aware of what is going on inside of you. Encourage yourself rather than beat yourself up for being tense. Evaluate your self-talk when you are stressed. For example, if you are stuck on the highway and can't move, what you say to yourself determines how you feel. You will be stressed if you say, " *How stupid of me to come this way. I should have listened to the traffic report so I* would have known not to come this way." Instead say, "I don't like that I am stuck in this traffic, but there is nothing I can do, so I might as well relax. Look at the angry people in that car." Maybe that can help you laugh and experience less stress.

Remember that you don't want to try to eliminate all stress. A certain amount is healthy. If you had no stress, you probably would be doing so little you wouldn't enjoy life. The challenge is to convert this stress to work for you rather than against you.

SELF EVALUATION:

1. What are the signs when I am stressed?

    a. I feel overwhelmed.
    b. I have trouble doing anything.
    c. I am short-tempered.
    d. I yell at the children.
    e. I get angry easier.

2. Beliefs I could use in regard to my stress:

    a. Everyone deserves to relax, including me.
    b. I do make mistakes, but I also do most things right.
    c. I need to fit a relaxation time in my busy schedule.

3. Action I could take to become less stressed:

    a. Listen to relaxing tapes.
    b. Take a warm bath with candles and soft music.
    c. Set priorities for what I have to do and let the rest go, so I won't get overwhelmed.

EXERCISES:

1. Before an event at which you expect to be stressed, visualize what may take place. Then visualize how you can react in a less stressful way. When the event occurs, you will have prepared yourself to react the way you wanted.

2. Be kind to yourself during a tense situation. Don't dwell on the poor aspects of your performance. Dwell on what you did well and what you accomplished.

3. After the tense situation, relax and celebrate it being over. This will give you a new sense of energy.

4. For additional help, read <u>Type E Woman. How to Overcome Stress of Being Everything to Everybody</u> by Harriet Braiken.

Relaxation Techniques

On a daily basis, relaxation techniques help you relax and prevent you from eating when stressed. When you're stressed, you eat faster, you eat more, and don't enjoy the food. When you are relaxed, you eat slower and taste the food rather than gulp it down. Use your body to help you get in touch with your stresses.

BODY PART	EXERCISE
Hands and Forearms	*Clench fists into ball. Next, spread fingers wide and bend hand backwards.*
Biceps	*Flex biceps into hard, tight muscle.*
Triceps	*Extend arms straight while tensing triceps.*

BODY PART	EXERCISE
Stomach	*Push stomach out, tensing all stomach muscles. Tighten stomach and suck it in.*
Mouth	*Stretch your mouth around your teeth, tensing mouth and cheek muscles. Repeat five times.*
Neck and Throat	*Roll neck slowly seven times to the right. Then roll your neck seven times to the left. Drive chin toward the chest, tensing all neck muscles.*
Shoulders	*Drive shoulders up toward ear lobes. Drop shoulders. Repeat five times.*
Buttocks	*Clench buttocks tightly together. Relax buttocks. Repeat five times.*
Thighs	*Lift feet slightly off the ground and tense thigh muscles.*
Calf Muscles	*Point toes up toward ceilings and drive heels down toward the floor while you tense your calf muscles.*

1. **What do I do to relax?**
2. **What are forms of relaxation that I would enjoy?**

   a. Learn yoga.
   b. Get a massage.
   c. Get a back rub.
   d. Read a book.
   e. Listen to music.
   f. See a movie or play.

3. **What are my greatest stresses?**

   a. My weight and eating.
   b. Lack of money.
   c. My relationship with spouse, children, friends.

4. **What could I do to lessen my stresses?**

   a. Speak up for what I need at work.
   b. Not take everything so seriously.
   c. Discuss rather than argue.

5. **What is the relationship of stress in my life and my eating?**

   a. The more stressed I am, the less I eat because of my need for control. (Anorexic)
   b. I get a sense of relief after I throw up. (Bulimic)
   c. I overeat to numb myself from the stress. (Binge eater)

EXERCISES:

1. Use any of the following techniques prior to eating. When you are tense, identify what is bothering you at that moment. Smile and say to yourself, *"I am not going to let this bother my body. I am going to protect my body."*

2. Scan your body to sense your tense or uncomfortable spots (stomach, head, and shoulders). Loosen this area up a little by tensing and then relaxing the area.

3. Switch your thoughts to your breathing. Take two deep breaths from your abdomen through your nose and exhale slowly through your mouth. As you exhale the second breath, let your jaw go limp. You can take a break and use this technique at work to help you relax.

4. Hold each muscle group in a tensed position for ten seconds and then relax it for 45-60 seconds. Repeat with one muscle group before going to the next muscle group. Tense the muscle group tightly, but not so tight as to create pain. It is important that each muscle group is as relaxed as the previous group before proceeding to the next group. If it is not, complete additional tension-relaxation cycles until that particular muscle group is completely relaxed. At the end of the exercise, scan your body. Repeat tensing and relaxing any muscle group until it is tension free. This is also a great technique to use when you have trouble sleeping.

5. For further help, read Relaxation and Stress Reduction Workbook by Davis, Eshelman, and McKay.

Play (Have Fun)

Some of my clients have never learned to play or have fun as children, so they don't know how to play as adults. Many were responsible for younger siblings, which prevented them from being a child. Some were children of alcoholics who kept secrets and were afraid to have other children around for fear of what they would see. It often made the child feel responsible for the irresponsible drunk adult.

Many anorexics find it difficult to allow themselves to play and have fun. They are so preoccupied with control in their lives it interferes with their ability to let loose and have fun. Many bulimics and binge eaters do know how to have fun, but don't often give themselves the opportunity to do so.

When was the last time you had fun, laughed, or allowed yourself to play? You may ask yourself, what could you do as an adult to play or have fun? Do what you did as a child. If you enjoy sports, you may like camping, boating, riding a bike, skiing, swimming, or dancing. If you are artistic, you might enjoy painting, writing, playing an instrument, creating art, or going to plays and museums. Observe children's actions and think about what you would enjoy doing. Let the child within have a great time; she wants to play. It is never too late to learn how to have fun. When you have fun, you replace the void you have been filling up with food with a healthier alternative.

SELF EVALUATION:

1. **When was the last time you played or had fun? What did you previously do that you could do again? What does the child in you want to do that you don't allow it to do?**

    a. *Wants to be more spontaneous rather than so controlled.*
    b. *Wants to sing as loudly as possible.*
    c. *Wants to go to the park and swing, run, and act as I did when I was a child.*
    d. *I haven't played since I was a child.*
       (You will feel much better when you allow yourself to play.)

2. **What beliefs could you have that would allow you to have fun and play?**

    a. *There is time for work and play.*
    b. *All work and no play makes one stressed and boring.*
    c. *Children and adults have the right to play and have fun.*
    d. *No matter how large I am I have the right to play and have fun.*

3. **My eating is related to my not having fun by:**

    a. *I am afraid that if I play and have fun, I will lose control of my eating. (Anorexic)*
    b. *I use eating as my way to have fun because I don't play.*
    c. *When I have fun and am playful, I don't overeat.*

EXERCISES:

1. Visualize yourself playing and having fun. What are ways you could have fun? On a scale of 1-10, how does it feel?

2. Journal other thoughts and feelings in regard to your playing and having fun.

3. For additional help, read <u>Dance Naked in Your Living Room: Handling Stress and Finding Joy</u> by Rebecca Ruggles Radcliff.

Stress Journal

Choose a major situation that made you unhappy and stressed. Think in terms of how you could change the situation to make it less stressful. What are the roadblocks keeping you from changing? What are your resources that you can draw on to change?

DATE:

Monday, June 5, 1997 12:30 p.m.

SITUATION (WHO, WHAT, WHEN, WHERE?):

I was ready to go to lunch with the other workers in my office when my supervisor asked me to type a three page letter that she needed right away. I didn't want to do it until I got back from lunch, but she said she needed it now. I was hungry and upset that I couldn't go to lunch as planned with my friends.

PHYSICAL REACTIONS (TIGHTNESS, FROWN, RAPID BREATHING):

My face and neck turned red because I was angry. My voice was shaky when I told her I would like to write the letter after lunch. My heart was racing as I spoke. I felt light-headed.

EMOTIONS (FEAR, ANGER, ANXIETY, GUILT)

I was angry, upset, and anxious that I had to give up my lunch hour to type her paper.

THOUGHTS (SELF-TALK TO SELF AND OTHERS):

I thought if I didn't get the paper done right away, she would fire me.

RESPONSE:

My lack of response made me feel worse.

BEHAVIORS (GRIT TEETH, CLINCH FISTS, SHOUT):

I tensed up, my shoulders were tight, I made mistakes in my typing and got light-headed from not eating so I ate three candy bars.

BEHAVIORS I COULD HAVE CHANGED:

I could have told her that it was unfair for her to ask me at the last minute. I could have stated I wanted to do a good job for her and I knew I could not perform when I was hungry. Instead of eating three candy bars, I could have eaten a nutritious snack until I went to lunch.

POSSIBLE SOLUTIONS:

I could have done it an hour later than what she requested since the mail was not picked up until 3:00.

Find a Balance in Your Life

In order to lessen your stress, feel good about yourself and to lead a healthy life, you need to find balance in your life. Balances keep us centered and in control. There are many ways we need to balance our lives. The following are ways you may want to make sure your life is balanced.

Balance my Life

BEHAVIOR	USUAL PRACTICE (1-10)	ACTION TO TAKE (1-10)
Work vs. Play	*I work so many hours I have little time to play. (1)*	*Work my 40 hours at work and then leave it. When not at work, do playful things. (9)*
Serious vs. Fun Times	*I am much too serious, which makes me boring to others. (1)*	*Make sure I have fun time as a priority. Allow for at least one fun thing to do daily. (9)*
Balance Food From Food Pyramid Group	*I eat much too many sweets and fats. (1)*	*Follow the food plan to make sure I get the right amount from each of the food groups. (9)*
Active vs. Quiet Times	*I have too much time sitting and not enough active time. (2)*	*Allow myself time to be active so that I don't get depressed. (9)*
Thinking vs. Feelings	*I always think and deny what I feel. (3)*	*Ask what I feel, not what I think. (7)*

BEHAVIOR	USUAL PRACTICE (1-10)	ACTION TO TAKE (1-10)
Challenged Thinking vs. Relaxed Thoughts	*I do so much computer work. I do not balance my time with creative and relaxed time.* (2)	*Allow myself time to write creatively. Read books or watch television programs I enjoy.* (9)
Time Alone vs. Time with Others	*I rarely have any time alone. I crave it.* (1)	*Take the phone off the hook, take my children to the sitters, and enjoy time by myself.* (9)
Time with Family vs. Work	*I spend too much time at work. When I get home I am too tired to do anything with my family.* (2)	*Get energy and satisfactions from my family by spending more time with them.* (9)
Time with Family vs. Friends	*I rarely spend time with my friends.* (1)	*Go out with my friends at least one to two times a month. Make sure I allow sufficient time for my family.* (9)

BEHAVIOR	USUAL PRACTICE (1-10)	ACTION TO TAKE (1-10)
Passive vs. Assertive Times	*I rarely am passive. I am always trying to get things done.* (2)	*Give myself permission to be passive. Listen and learn from other people.* (9)
Feminine vs. Masculine Traits	*I do not allow my feminine traits to be shown.* (3)	*I can be more sensitive, loving and caring which will make me like myself better.* (8)
Spiritual Times vs. Other Times	*I have not been going to church lately. I miss the spiritual closeness of my higher power and my church friends.* (2)	*Start going to my place of worship. Start a new relationship with my higher power.* (8)
Aggressive vs. Assertive	*I am aggressive which turns people off.* (2)	*Be assertive by telling what I feel.* (8)

SELF EVALUATION:

1. **What are the ways I provide balance in my life?**

   a. *I balance my work and play.*
   b. *I balance my quiet and active times.*
   c. *I balance my time alone and with friends.*

2. **What are ways in which my life is unbalanced?**

   a. *I isolate myself too much.*
   b. *I don't have enough time to play or relax.*
   c. *Life is too serious for me.*

3. **Models in my life who have shown me how to balance or unbalance my life:**

   a. *Parents worked all the time and had little time to play.*
   b. *My whole family was not social enough.*
   c. *My parents did not know how to handle their stress.*
   d. *My family works too much and doesn't play enough.*

EXERCISES:

1. Use the chart above and write where your life is balanced and unbalanced. What action do you need to take to have your life balanced?

2. Visualize yourself having balance in your life in an area you feel most unbalanced. Imagine yourself balancing that aspect of your life. What are you doing differently?

3. Write thoughts and feelings about balancing your life. Make some goals to see that it happens.

4. For additional help, read <u>Appetites: On Search for True Nourishment</u> by Genee Roth.

Stress/Relaxed Evaluation

BEHAVIOR	USUAL PATTERN (1-10)	ACTION TO TAKE (1-10)
Awareness of Stress	*I have no idea when I am stressed until I get physically ill.* *(2)*	*Take a biofeedback class to become aware of my stress.* *(9)*
Types of Stress	*Work, money, partner, sex, and family.* *(3)*	*Choose and work on one stress at a time.* *(9)*
Muscle Relaxation	*I am so tense from not relaxing.* *(2)*	*Each day relax my muscles.* *(9)*
Relaxation Techniques	*I do not use any relaxation techniques.* *(2)*	*Give myself at least an hour a day for time to relax.* *(9)*
Play and Have Fun	*I never play or have any fun.* *(1)*	*I am going to go on a vacation.* *(9)*

CHAPTER TEN

Enrich Your Career to Change Your Weight and Self-esteem

When you hate your job, it's understandable that you need to find other sources of pleasure. Eating often becomes that pleasure. If you hate your job, change it. If you don't know what you would like to do, take the Campbell Interest Inventory or other personality or interest inventories. These tests are available at career centers at colleges or universities.

When we are unhappy with work, it is understandable that we want to compensate and find other pleasures outside our jobs. Many people have said they binge when they come home from work. They feel the need to reward themselves with food for getting through the day. It gives them something to look forward to after a dismal day on the job.

I was anorexic for a short time when I hated my job. I have always been happy with my work except for the year and a half that I licensed day care centers. I hated to be the "bad guy" who closed centers and see personnel who abused children. Since I hated my job, I had to work very hard to find pleasures outside my work. I became obsessed with my weight. I didn't eat and I couldn't be thin enough. Once I went back to university teaching and was challenged, I didn't have the time or interest to obsess about my weight.

■■■

Career Analysis

Since you spend much of your time at your job, it is important you are in the right career. If you are not happy, challenged, or rewarded the way you'd like to be, then think about how you can change the job to make it better or how you can get a different job. It is important to choose a career that best meets your needs. You need to determine what is the most important part of your career. How much money do you need to make? How important is prestige to you? What provides you with a sense of satisfaction? Do you like to work alone or with people? Do you need to be your own boss or work for someone? What are your skills and strengths?

Unfortunately, many people feel stuck in a career they do not enjoy because of economic pressures. A change would cost them too much money. But, if you don't enjoy the work, you may want to re-evaluate if it is healthy for you to remain in this job.

SELF EVALUATION:

1. What do you like about your job? Dislike about it?

> a. *I don't like my boss.*
> b. *I do like my co-workers.*
> c. *It is challenging.*

2. What can you change? How do you make this change happen?

> a. *I can rewrite my job description as I'd like it. I could present it to my boss for her approval.*
> b. *I can become more creative so my job is not repetitive.*
> c. *Ask to be transferred to a new department so I can have something new to do, which would be more challenging.*

3. What are your fears in making a change?

> a. *I will miss the people I work with now.*
> b. *I'm afraid I won't like the new job.*
> c. *I've been there for so long, it is hard to make a change.*

234

4. **What are the beliefs that you could use to make your career better for you?**

   a. *When I am in a job that is not using my strengths, I would be more satisfied if I changed jobs.*
   b. *I deserve to be in a meaningful and challenging job.*
   c. *It is my right to speak up for what I want.*

5. **How does my eating relate to my career?**

   a. *When I get home from my job I hate, I am so tired all I want to do is relax by eating.*
   b. *When I am frustrated with my career, I get angry and stuff my feelings with food.*
   c. *I feel I am discriminated against because I am fat. (It is against the law to be discriminated because of your weight.)*

EXERCISES:

1. Visualize yourself in your ideal career and job situation. Imagine the work you would do, the work environment, the opportunity to be yourself and everything you want from the job. Go for it.

2. Journal other thoughts or feelings in regard to your career.

3. For additional help, read What Color is Your Parachute? by Richard Bolles.

Maximize Your Strengths and Minimize Your Weaknesses

We all have strengths and weaknesses. Too often we think about our weaknesses without giving a thought to our strengths. When we do this, we don't give ourselves enough credit. We can benefit greatly if we develop our strengths rather than use all of our energy focusing on our weaknesses. Don't waste your time on your weaknesses, which leads to frustration. Instead, use your energy to improve your strengths. You will feel better about yourself because you are dealing with your strong areas.

Anorexics, bulimics, and binge eaters are great examples of people who dwell on their weaknesses and ignore their strengths. They will focus all of their energy on their body and weight while overlooking the other important aspects of their being.

Following is a list of common personality characteristics that influences what kind of career is best for you. It is important to choose a career that best suits your personality and strengths. Underline those descriptions that best describe you. Then have a supervisor or someone who knows you well circle those characteristics she believes best describes you. Cross out your weaknesses since you are not going to dwell on them.

Strengths

Accepting	Congenial	Genuine	Organized
Achieving	Conscientious	Good-natured	Outgoing
Active	Considerate	Graceful	Patient
Adventurous	Cooperative	Helpful	Perceptive
Affectionate	Creative	Humorous	Persistent
Ambitious	Dependable	Happy	Reassuring
Articulate	Determined	Independent	Self-confident
Assertive	Energetic	Insightful	Sociable
Caring	Entertaining	Intelligent	Spontaneous
Charming	Enthusiastic	Intuitive	Thoughtful
Cheerful	Friendly	Likeable	Trusting
Compassion	Gentle	Open-minded	Warm

SELF EVALUATION:

1. **Look at what are the discrepancies between how you and your friend view you. Ask your friend what they perceive as your weaknesses. What would you think of someone who has all the qualities that your friend described you? Begin to internalize these traits. You are more than what you weigh. The above exercise indicates this to be true.**

236

2. **List other qualities that describe your strengths and weaknesses.**

   a. Strengths: *Dependable, fun, intelligent, and sensitive.*
   b. Weaknesses: *Controlled and inability to be flexible*

3. **Beliefs I have which keep me from feeling good about my strengths include:**

   a. *It is more important to think of how to improve myself than it is to give myself credit for what I do well.*
   (You will never give yourself a break or feel content when you think this way.)

   b. *If I think of my strengths instead of my weaknesses, I'll never improve.*
   (When you think and act on your strengths, you will more than likely improve more than when you try to improve your weaknesses. Plus, it is a lot more fun to spend our energy on what we are good at than what we do poorly.)

4. **Beliefs I could use to further my strengths:**

   a. *If I spend more time thinking about my strengths and accept my weaknesses, I will feel better about myself.*
   b. *My strengths are an important part of my identity. My weaknesses also identify who I am, but I don't have to dwell on them.*
   c. *I can improve myself by spending more time on my strengths than my weaknesses. I will spend only the amount of time on my weaknesses that is absolutely necessary for me to do.*

5. **Action I can take to increase my strengths includes:**

   a. *Choose a career that interests me and takes advantage of my strengths.*
   b. *Talk to my supervisor about changing my job so I can do the things I do best.*
   c. *Take additional classes.*

6. Action I can take to overcome my weaknesses includes:

    a. Choose a career that doesn't require me to perform in my weakest areas.
    b. Observe others who have this area as their strength and recognize the difference in our personalities.
    c. Accept my weaknesses.

EXERCISES:

1. Visualize yourself feeling your strengths and not worried about your weaknesses. What does that feel like? Each time you get into your car, remind yourself of these strengths to help you feel good about yourself.

2. Journal thoughts and feelings in regard to your strengths and weaknesses. Make a list of your strengths and a list of your weaknesses. After each indicate the time you spend on each. Then write the amount of time you would like to spend. See the difference. What action do you need to take to spend more time on your strengths?

3. For additional help, read Where Do I Go From Here With My Life? by Richard Bolles.

Skills

    Below is a list of skills. Underline those skills that you think best describe yourself. Then have a co-worker, boss, or friend, circle those skills she believes best describe you. Give these skills the same importance that you do your weight and appearance. The result is you will feel better about yourself.

Act as liaison	Count	Humorous	Observant
Analyze	Design	Initiate	Organized
Classify	Entertain	Interview	Perceptive
Clarify	Evaluate	Make decisions	Proofread
Counsel	Expedite	Negotiate	Supervise

SELF EVALUATION:

1. **What are the differences between how I perceive myself and how my co-worker or a friend perceives me? What do I think of a person who has these circled traits?**
(Remember this is you.)

   a. *My friend was more positive than I was.*
   b. *I didn't know I was perceived to have that many skills.*
   c. *Maybe I am not as awful as I thought.*

2. **What are other skills that I have?**

   a. *Aware of details.*
   b. *Good with people.*
   c. *Dependable and reliable.*
   d. *Computer skills.*

3. **What beliefs do I have that keep me from believing in myself?**

   a. *It is not right to feel proud.*
      (It is important that you are proud of your skills. This doesn't mean you have to put others down.)

   b. *My parents said I was a nobody.*
      (How does it benefit you to continue to think this way?)

   c. *I don't believe I can do anything right.*
      (No one is good at everything they try.)

4. **How can I change my beliefs so I believe in myself?**

   a. *I will start to look at my strengths instead of dwelling on my mistakes.*
   b. *I no longer think of myself as a nobody. I am proud of who I am and what I am able to achieve.*
   c. *I can think of the positive things I do instead of thinking of what I do poorly.*

5. How are my skills used in the present job that I have?

    a. *I don't use my skills at all where I am now employed. No wonder I hate my job.*
    (Think about how much better you will feel about yourself when you have a job, which uses your skills.)

    b. *I use most of my skills in my present job except the two that are the most important to me.*
    (How can you make this happen?)

    c. *I have never thought about what my skills are. I know that my co-workers like working with me.*
    (Good. You are now thinking about what you do well instead of what you do poorly. That's what you want to do.)

6. How does not using my skills influence my eating?

    a. *When I use my skills, I have less need to eat.*
    b. *When I don't use my skills, I become frustrated and overeat.*
    c. *When my skills are not appreciated, I overeat.*
    d. *When others don't value my skills, I don't want to try to do my best.*
    e. *When I work using my skills, I don't even think about my weight or food.*

EXERCISES:

1. Visualize yourself in a career that emphasizes your skills. On a scale of 1-10, how does that feel? What do you need to do to have this happen?

2. Journal other thoughts and feelings about your skills. Once you define what are your skills, decide what kind of career best fits with those skills. Is your career now allowing you to use your skills?

3. For additional help, read Passages by Gail Sheehy.

Learn from Past Successes and Failures

Do you stay in a career you dislike because you fear no one would hire you because of your weight? You don't need to use your weight to keep you from changing jobs. To be successful in your career, it is important to look at past successes and failures. See if you can detect a pattern in what has helped in your successes or what contributed to your failures. Do you have problems with leadership, getting along with others, or being insubordinate? Do you need to be in charge, independent, creative, or do you need to be motivated? More people are fired because of their interactions with others, not because of their job performance.

If you are reliable, you do what you say. Most people with an eating problem are reliable. In fact, many companies don't want their employees to get treatment for their eating disorders because they are good employees. They will do anything to be on the good side of the boss. Some will work overtime without pay or do two people's jobs for the pay of one. Most will do whatever others ask, no matter how unfair the request is. This does not help the employee's eating problem. Once they get away from the hectic work, food becomes a retreat. They feel they have been so good at the job they feel they deserve a treat, which is often non-stop bingeing.

I don't suggest you be unreliable. Reliability is an important quality. Just because you are reliable doesn't mean you must do anything asked of you. You have the right to speak up for what is fair and expect respect from others.

SELF EVALUATION:

1. What have been your career successes in the past?

a. I was good manager.
b. I never called in sick.
c. I was good with details.
d. I related well to my co-workers.
e. Everyone enjoyed working with me.
f. I was competent at what I did.
g. I made lots of money.

2. What failures on the job have you experienced in the past?

   a. *Told I was too bossy.*
   b. *Too moody.*
   c. *Too slow.*

3. What are your fears of success?

   a. *I will be expected to continue at that level and I'm afraid I can't.*
   b. *I will later fail at what I'm successful at now.*
   c. *I am afraid I can't be successful because I never have been.*
   d. *I am comfortable with failure because it is what I know.* (This is often true when you first experience success. Once you start to feel comfortable with success, you will not feel as comfortable with failure.)

4. What are your fears of failing?

   a. *I will disappoint others.*
   b. *I will look like a fool.*
   c. *Mistakes will mean I will get fired.*

5. What action can you take to have successes?

   a. *Plan what I want to have happen and take steps to see that it happens.*
   b. *Develop my strengths and do things I want to do.*
   c. *Take the Myers Briggs Type Indicator to identify my personality so I choose a career according to it.*

6. How is my eating related to my successes and failures?

   a. *When I fail, I starve myself to make up for the mistake. (Anorexic)*
   b. *When I am successful, I do not have the urge to purge. (Bulimic)*
   c. *When I have a success, I eat to celebrate. (Binge eater)*

242

EXERCISES:

1. Visualize yourself as successful. What must you do to achieve it? YOU CAN DO IT! Good luck.

2. Write your feelings and thoughts about your successes and failures. See if you can see a pattern. What does that tell you that you need to do in order to succeed?

3. For additional reading, read <u>Deadly Diet: Recovering from Anorexia and Bulimia</u> by Terence Sandbeck or <u>Overcoming Fear of Success</u> by Martha Friedman.

Parenting: Your Career?

How you feel as a parent to your children may influence your eating habits. If you are frustrated with your attempts at parenting, you may turn to food for a reward for what you feel is a thankless job. If your parents were not there for you, you are at a distinct disadvantage because you don't have a good parental role to model. You only know what not to do. You must make a special effort to be different and not make the mistakes your parents made. You can break the dysfunctional cycle with parenting classes, awareness, and effort. If you had wonderful parents, it will be much easier for you to parent. You can repeat what your parents did for you.

If full-time parenting isn't rewarding for you, you and your children will benefit if you take a part-or full-time job. It is not the quantity, but the quality of time that makes the difference for your children. You can't give to others if you do not fulfill your needs.

Anorexics often find parenting with small children difficult because of their need for order and cleanliness. Bulimics and binge eaters are often very nurturing people who enjoy giving to their children.

SELF EVALUATION:

1. What are my needs about parenting and a career?

    a. I need to stay home with my children.
    b. I need part-time work.
    c. I want to stay home but I can't afford to do so.
       (Have you thought about what kind of job you could do which allows you to stay home?)

2. What changes would be helpful for me to make?

    a. I need to find a job. My children are driving me crazy.
    b. I need more stimulation than staying at home.
    c. I need to quit my work. I want to be home with my children.

3. Action I can take to become a better parent:

    a. Find time for me to feel good about myself so I have something to give to my children. Give them quality time.
    b. Read parenting books or attend parenting classes to learn how to become a better parent.
    c. Treat my children the way I wanted to be treated as a child.

4. Beliefs that would help me become a better parent:

    a. Children need to be respected rather than owned.
    b. As a parent, I need to help my children learn to assume responsibility for their actions.
    c. If I listen to my children, they can be helpful in helping me understand what they need.

5. Eating is related to my parenting:

    a. Parenting drains me so I turn to food to give me energy.
    b. Eating seems to be the only pleasure I have.
    c. When I get stressed with my children, I turn to food for relief.
    d. I overeat when I do not get to spend enough time with my children.

EXERCISES:

1. Visualize yourself as a full-time parent or having a part-or full-time job. On a scale of 1-10, how does it feel to be able to spend the amount of time you wish with your children?

2. Journal other thoughts and feeling in regard to you being a parent.

3. For additional help, read <u>Parent Effectiveness Training</u> by Tom Gordon.

Workaholic

Workaholics are often those who work in order not to have to have intimate relationships or deal with their feelings. They try to prove their love for their families by being good providers and are unaware their families would rather have quality time together.

Their addictive behaviors continue and they are lonely and isolated from the families they desperately need. Workaholics are not people pleasers and they internally drive themselves to advance. There are more male workaholics than females. This is usually because males often have more of their identity wrapped up in their career. Females are generally more involved in their relationships. Many times the spouse of a person with an eating disorder is a workaholic. She turns to food since her spouse is not around to meet her emotional needs. The following are work habits that may fit you or your workaholic spouse: *

1.	I put more energy into my work than into my relationships.
2.	I always seem to be in a hurry.
3.	It is hard for me to relax and enjoy myself except when I am at work.
4.	I get upset when I am not in control.
5.	I get impatient when I have to wait for anyone to get his work done.
6.	I spend more energy on the future than the here and now.

245

7. I get upset when I make any mistake.
8. Things do not get done fast enough for me.
9. I feel guilty when I am not working.
10. My greatest pleasures are at work.
11. I find I am the last person to leave work.
12. My final project is more important to me than the process.
13. My identity is tied to my work.

* Reprinted in part from <u>Overdoing It: How To Slow Down and Take Care Of Yourself</u> by Bryan Robinson, Health Communications, ©1992.

SELF EVALUATION:

1. Reasons I am a workaholic:

> *a. To make enough money to support my family.*
> *b. In order to avoid my partner who is always getting on my case about my weight.*
> *c. So I don't have to deal with my partner who gets on my nerves if I am around her too much.*
> *d. I am trying to prove I am good at my work.*
> *e. Work is the only place I get any gratification.*
> *f. Since my spouse works all the time, I figure I might as well do the same.*
> *g. When I work a lot, I have less problems controlling my eating.*

2. My workaholic behavior is related to the following beliefs:

> *a. My work identifies who I am. Thus, the more I work, the more important I am.*
> *b. If I don't overwork, I will overeat.*
> *c. Since I am overweight, I need to compensate for my looks.*
> *d. The more I work, the more I will be appreciated.*
> (The quality of your work is more valued than the time you spend.)

3. **Beliefs I could substitute for my workaholic behavior:**

   a. *I am more than my work. My work is a part of my identity, but not my entire identity.*
   b. *I can cut down on the amount of time I work and replace that time with new hobbies and interests instead of overeating.*
   c. *Although I am overweight, I do not have to overwork.*

4. **Action I could take to overcome my work addiction:**

   a. *Spend less time at work and find new pleasures.*
   b. *Do more things with my partner, family, or friends.*
   c. *Tell my supervisor I am exhausted working the number of hours I now work and need to work less.*

5. **My eating is related to my work addiction:**

   a. *When I am hungry and haven't eaten, I don't perform as well on the job.*
   b. *When I overwork, I purge. (Bulimic)*
   c. *When I work too much, I overeat. (Binge eater)*
   d. *When I am unhappy with my work, I turn to food for pleasure.*

EXERCISES:

1. Visualize you or your partner no longer being a workaholic. On a scale of 1-10, how does that feel? What do you need to do to see that this visualization comes true?

2. Write in your journal thoughts and feelings about you or your partner's workaholic behavior. Practice saying what you need to say to your workaholic spouse after writing the letter.

3. For additional help read Overdoing It: How To Slow Down And Take Care Of Yourself by Bryan Robinson.

Set Realistic Goals

In order to be successful with your career and your weight, it is important that you set realistic goals. There is nothing wrong with long-term goals, as long as you also have some short-term goals that are achievable. When you think of losing one hundred pounds, you feel overwhelmed. However, if you break this down to losing one pound per week, you are more realistic. When you expect to become president of a company without beginning at a lower level, you may have set yourself up for a failure. In setting goals, imagine and visualize what you want so you can achieve it. Focused direction produces focused results. It is essential to know what you want in order to get there. Your visualization will include your dreams, but it must also include your needs.

SELF EVALUATION:

1. List of my dreams:

   a. To be independently wealthy so I can retire at forty.
   b. Own my own business.
   c. Have 50 people working for me.
   d. To be famous.
   e. To be the best.

2. List of my needs:

   a. To be wealthy enough to pay my bills.
   b. To be my own boss.
   c. To be in charge.
   d. I need to be recognized for what I do well.

3. Resources I have (assets in personality traits, friends, financial resources, education, time and energy) to reach my goals:

   a. I am smart and have my Ph.D.
   b. I have 20 years of experience in my career.
   c. I have lots of friends and support.

4. Changes I need to make to achieve my goals:

    a. Tell myself I deserve to reach my goals.
    b. Be realistic in what I can achieve.
    c. Stop procrastinating and get started.
    d. Ask myself what do I want to do and how do I get there.
       Then go for it.
    e. Take a small step at a time.
       (First take a small step which you can have success. Then
       choose another small step. You want successes, not failures.)

5. My eating and weight are related to my career goal setting:

    a. When I don't reach my goals, I overeat.
    b. I sabotage myself by expecting too much of myself and then
       turn to food to feel better.
    c. When I overeat, I feel as if I am not worthy to pursue my
       career goals.
    d. When I eat properly, I feel better, and have more energy
       to achieve my goals.

EXERCISES:

1. Visualize yourself accomplishing your goals. Take one goal at a time and decide how you can reach it. Repeat with your next goal.

2. Make a list of your dreams and needs. Then indicate what action you need to take to have your dreams come true.

3. List your eating, personal, and career goals for today, a week, a month, a year, and the next five years. Use the table below as a guide.

4. For additional help, read Success is Quality of Your Journal by Jennifer James.

Goals

EATING GOALS	
Today	*Write down everything I eat so I am conscious of what I eat.*
Week	*Eat slowly at each meal for the week. Lose a pound a week.*
Month	*Write what I eat following the food pyramid guide until I know it.*
Year	*Have each of the above goals as a habit. Lose 50 pounds for the year.*
5 Years	*Continue eating healthy. Maintain my weight loss.*
PERSONAL GOALS	
Today	*Do at least one fun thing today. Go out for lunch, read a book.*
Week	*Do at least seven things for me this week, including getting a massage.*
Month	*Continue to treat myself daily with an activity I enjoy. Exercise at least 20 times during the month.*

CAREER GOALS	
Today	*Write a resume.*
Week	*Send out resumes to 20 perspective jobs.*
Month	*Follow up the resume with 20 phone calls. Quit old job to start my new job.*
Year	*Get a promotion with more pay, responsibility, and prestige.*
5 Years	*Start my own business.*
OTHER GOALS	
Week	*Go to church.*
Month	*Volunteer to feed the needy.*
Year	*Learn to ski.*
5 Years	*Get married.*

Career Evaluation

SITUATION	USUAL PATTERN (1-10)	ACTION TO TAKE (1-10)
Career Analysis	*I hate my job. I think I'm in the wrong career. (1)*	*I need to go back to school and get a degree in what I want to do. (9)*
Career Strengths	*My present job doesn't deal with people, which is my greatest strength. (1)*	*Find a job or career where I deal with people instead of with a computer. (9)*
Career Weaknesses	*I see the big picture, but am horrible when it comes to paying attention to details. (2)*	*Have someone do the detail part of my job. Then I can concentrate on what I like to do. (9)*
Career Successes	*I have had little success in my career. (1)*	*I have been asked to stay on jobs when I have quit. (9)*

252

SITUATION	USUAL PATTERN (1-10)	ACTION TO TAKE (1-10)
Career Failures	*I always get fired because I am late.* (2)	*Find a job where I have flexible hours.* (9)
Skills	*My career doesn't allow me to work on a computer, which is my greatest love and skill.* (2)	*Find a job where I can use my computer skills.* (9)
Workaholic	*I work two jobs so I don't have time to think or feel.* (2)	*I am going to quit one job and work only 40 hours.* (9)
Parenting as a Career	*I hate working.* (2)	*I'm going to find a job which allows me to work at home.* (9)
Goals	*I never set goals. I have no direction in my life.* (2)	*Set a goal for a day. Next, set a goal for a month, a year, and five years. Be realistic so I can meet my goals.* (8)

Characteristics of Anorexia Nervosa

Check the characteristics that describe you. You may want to look at your checks as areas for you to make some changes.

1.	Restricting type: Not regularly engaging in binge-eating or purging behavior, but regularly starves self.
2.	Binge-eating type: Regularly engages in binge eating or purging.
3.	Refuses to maintain minimally normal body weight for age and weight (less than 85 percent of that expected).
4.	Intense fear of gaining weight or becoming fat, even though underweight.
5.	Distorted body image: Denial of the seriousness of the current low body weight. Sees self as fat.
6.	The absence of at least three consecutive menstrual cycles.
7.	Thinking requires perfection: Sees black-and-white and no grays
8.	Control is very important; difficulty in being flexible.
9.	Enjoys feeding others, even though does not eat with them.
10.	Exercises extensively until too weak.
11.	Obsessive thinking. Fun and laughter missing.
12.	Very bright and intelligent. Successful in career.
13.	Unaware of feelings: Often appears without emotions.
14.	Families appear to be perfect, but are denying problems.
15.	Mothers enmeshed with daughters.
16.	Fathers are emotionally isolated from daughters.
17.	Described by parents as a perfect daughter until anorexia began.
18.	Very competitive with others. Master in manipulating others.
19.	Isolated from others, rarely involved in romantic relationship.
20.	Very independent. Refuses help from others.
21.	Identity related to how thin you are.
22.	Strong moral values and rigid sense of what is right and wrong.
23.	Feels asexual as result of hatred of body.

Characteristics of Bulimia Nervosa

Check those characteristics that describe you. Look at your checks as areas for you to make some changes.

1.	Recurrent episodes of binge eating.
2.	Eating an amount of food that is definitely larger than most people would eat during similar period of time.
3.	Binge eating and purging occurs, on average at least twice a week for three months.
4.	Purging includes self-induced vomiting or the misuses of laxatives, diuretics, or enemas.
5.	Usually within 10 pounds of ideal weight.
6.	Body shape and weight unduly influence self-evaluation.
7.	Obsessive in thinking about food, weight, body, and purging.
8.	Emotional. Feel as if your feelings are out of control.
9.	Thinking is negative.
10.	May be excessive in exercise.
11.	Families are often explosive and out-of-control.
12.	May have previous history of alcohol or drug abuse.
13.	Often depressed.
14.	Feels guilty about secret of purging. Lies about purging.
15.	Shoplifts.
16.	People-pleasers. Unaware of how to take care of own needs.
17.	Co-dependent or dependent on approval from others.
18.	Confused boundary issues.
19.	Lack of support systems.
20.	Low self-esteem. Hates self for purging.
21.	Identity revolved around eating, body size, and purging.
22.	Promiscuous.
23.	Victim of sexual abuse.
24.	Lack of assertive skills. Manipulated by others.
25.	Uses purging as means for relaxing. Lacks relaxation skills.

Characteristics of a Binge Eater

Check those characteristics that describe you. You may want to look at your checks as areas for you to make some changes.

1.	Recurrent episodes of binge eating.
	a. Sense of lack of control over eating. Feeling that you can't stop eating.
	b. Binge eating occurs without self-induced vomiting or misuse of laxatives, diuretics, or enemas.
2.	Hatred of body.
3.	Overweight. Doesn't exercise.
4.	Obsessive in thinking about dieting and weight loss.
5.	Described by others as overly emotional.
6.	Stuffs feelings with food.
7.	Thinks negative about self, body, and weight.
8.	May have previous history of alcohol or drug abuse.
9.	Depression evident in self or family.
10.	Relationships may be abusive and lack intimacy.
11.	Families are uninvolved and critical.
12.	Helper of others; nurturing to others.
13.	Closer to fathers than mothers.
14.	Difficult to receive help from others.
15.	People pleasers. Unaware of how to please self.
16.	Co-dependent or dependent on others.
17.	Lack of confidence. Feels fat prevents success in career.
18.	Low self-esteem due to being overweight.
19.	Uses fat as protection of getting hurt.
20.	Disinterested in sex because of body size.
21.	Victim of physical or sexual abuse.
22.	Passive rather than assertive.
23.	Allows others to manipulate you. Difficult to say no.
24.	Lack of relaxation skills. Feels very stressed.

Tools

Check the following tools you now use. Next make a list of the tools you wish to start using.

I. Physical:
A. Follow the food guide pyramid.
B. Make lifetime changes in eating habits, not quick fixes.
C. Eat slowly. Chew your food slowly.
D. Limit the amount of fat in your daily diet.
E. Eat when physically hungry. Stop before you are full.
F. Stop depriving yourself. Think abundance.
G. Eat 3 meals plus 1-2 snacks daily.
H. Drink 8 glasses water daily.
I. Tell yourself you love your body when you think of food.
J. Start today to accept your body.
K. Stop the alcohol or drug abuse.
L. Have at least a yearly physical to check your electrolytes.
M. Use an anti-depressant to lessen depression, binge eating, and obsessive thinking when necessary.
N. Exercise moderately.
II. Intellectual:
A. Stop the distorted thinking.
B. Snap a rubber band on your wrist each time you use a negative or obsessive thought.
C. Give yourself permission to make mistakes.
D. Visualize yourself at your ideal weight to reach it.
E. Use daily affirmations.
III. Emotional:
A. Identify and express what you feel.
B. Journal write.
C. Grieve your losses.
D. Accept your feelings. Do not judge them as good or bad.
E. Do not stuff the feelings with food.
F. Give yourself permission to experience your feelings.

IV. Social:

   A. Develop healthy and intimate relationships.

   B. Identify what role your family plays in your eating issues.

   C. Balance time spent alone and with others.

   D. Stop trying to please other people when it is at your expense.

   E. Let go of control issues. Learn to negotiate.

   F. Set appropriate boundaries.

   G. Develop support systems.

V. Psychological:

   A. Accept and love yourself.

   B. Your identity is more than what you weigh.

   C. Love and accept the parent, adult, and child within.

   D. Enjoy the present.

VI. Spiritual:

   A. Develop a higher power.

   B. Forgive yourself and others. Be patience trustful, hopeful, courageous, honest and reliable.

VII. Sexual:

   A. Accept and enjoy your sexuality.

   B. Stop playing the victim role.

   C. Accept your femininity and masculinity traits.

VIII. Assertive:

   A. Be assertive rather than passive or aggressive.

   B. Say no.

   C. Send "I" messages instead of "you" blame messages.

   D. Avoid manipulating others or being manipulated.

IX. Stressed/Relaxed:

   A. Have fun. Play.

   B. Use relaxation techniques.

   C. Balance your life.

X. Career:

   A. Choose a career that uses your strengths.

   B. Set realistic goals.

B i b l i o g r a p h y

ASSERTIVE SELF

Alberti, Robert & Michael Emmons. <u>Your Perfect Right</u>. Impact
        Publishers, Inc., 1978 (third edition).
Smith, Manuel. <u>When I Say No, I Feel Guilty</u>. Bantam Books, 1977.

CAREER SELF

Bolles, Richard. <u>What Color is Your Parachute</u>? Ten Speed Press, 1970.
Robinson, Bryan. <u>Overdoing It: How To Slow Down and Take Care</u>
        <u>Of Yourself</u>. Health Communications, Inc., 1992.

EMOTIONAL SELF

Adams, Kay. <u>Journal to the Self</u>. Warner Books, 1990.
Berg, Francis. <u>Afraid to Eat. Children and Teens in Weight Crises</u>.
        Healthy Weight Journal, 1997.
Bourne, Edmund J. <u>The Anxiety and Phobia Workbook</u>. New Harbinger
        Publications, Inc., 1990.
Cohen, Mary Anne. <u>French Toast for Breakfast: Declaring Peace with</u>
        <u>Emotional Eating</u>. Gürze Books 1995.
Miirth, Meier, Hemfelt, Sneed and Hawkins. <u>Love Hunger: Recovery</u>
        <u>from Food Addiction</u>. Macmillan, 1970.
Roth, Geneen. <u>Feeding the Hungry Heart. The Experience of Compulsive</u>
        <u>Eating</u>. Bobbs-Merrill Co., Inc., 1982.
Roth, Geneen. <u>Why Weight? A Guide to Ending Compulsive Eating</u>.
        Plume Book, 1989.
Sundermeyer, Colleen. <u>Emotional Weight. Change Your Relationship</u>
        <u>with Food by Changing Your Relationship with Yourself</u>.
        Berkley Publishing Group, 1993.
Virtue, Doreen. <u>Losing Your Pounds of Pain</u>. Hay House, 1994.
Weisinger, Hendrie. <u>.Dr. Weisinger's Anger Work-out Book</u>.
        Quill, 1985.

INTELLECTUAL SELF

Adderholt-Elliot, Miriam. <u>Perfectionism: What's Bad about Being Too Good</u>? Free Spirit Publishing, 1987.
Burns, David. <u>Feeling Good</u>. Penguin Books, Inc., 1990.
Burns, David. <u>Feeling Good Handbook</u>. Penguin Books, Inc., 1994.
Crisp, Joughin, Halek, and Bowyer. <u>Anorexia Nervosa: The Wish to Change</u>. Harcourt Brace and Co. 1990.
Gawain, Shakti. <u>Creative Visualization</u>. Whatever Publishing, 1986.
Sandberg, Terence. <u>The Deadly Diet: Recovering from Anorexia and Bulimia</u>. New Harbinger Publication, 1996.
Stuart, Mary & Lynnzy Orr. <u>Otherwise Perfect. People and Their Problems with Weight</u>. Health Communications, Inc., 1987.
Ward, Susan. <u>Daily Affirmations for Compulsive Eaters. Beyond Feast and Famine</u>. Health Communications, 1990.

PHYSICAL SELF

Antonello, Jean. <u>Breaking Out of Food Jail</u>. Simon & Schuster, 1996.
Bruch, Hilde. <u>Conversations with Anorexics</u>. Basic Books Inc., 1988.
Cash, Thomas. <u>The Body Image Workbook. An 8 Step Program for Learning to Like Your Looks</u>. New Harbinger Publishers, 1997.
Dixon, Monica. <u>Love the Body You Were Born With: A 10-Step Workbook for Women</u>. Berkeley Publishing Group, 1996.
Fairburn, Christopher. <u>Overcoming Binge Eating</u>. Guilford Press, 1995.
Feedman, Rita. <u>Body Love: Learning to Like Our Looks and Ourselves</u>. Bowling Green Popular Press, 1989.
Foreyt and Goodrick. <u>Living Without Dieting</u>. Harrison Co., 1992.
Hall and Cohn. <u>Bulimia: Guide to Recovery: Understanding and Overcoming the Binge-Purge Syndrome</u>. Gürze Books, 1978.
Hall and Cohn. <u>Dear Kids of Alcoholics</u>. Gürze Books, 1988.
Hall and Cohn. <u>Recoveries: True Stories by People Who Conquered Addictions and Compulsions</u>. Gürze Books, 1987.
Hall, Lindsey.<u>Full Lives. Women Who Have Freed Themselves From Food and Weight Obsession</u>. Gürz Books, 1993.
Hirschmann, Jane & Carol H. Munter. <u>Overcoming Overeating. Living Free in a World of Food</u>. Addison-Wesley Publishing Inc., 1988.

261

Hirschmann and Munter. <u>When Women Stop Hating Their Bodies</u>. <u>Freeing Yourself From Food and Weight Obsession</u>. Fawett, 1995.

Hutchinson, Marcia Germaine. <u>Transforming Body Image</u>. The Crossing Press, 1988.

Johnston, Joni. <u>Appearance Obsession. Learning To Love the Way You Look</u>. Heath Communications, 1994.

Kano, Susan. <u>Making Peace With Food</u>. Harper/Collins, l985.

Katherine. Anne. <u>Anatomy of a Food Addiction</u>. Gürze Books, 1991.

Latimer, Jane E. <u>Living Binge-Free</u>. Living Quest, 1992.

Maine, Margo. <u>Father Hunger: Fathers, Daughters and Food</u>. Gürze Books, 1991.

Miller, Caroline. <u>My Name is Caroline</u>. Gürze Books, 1988.

Naidus, Beverly. <u>One Size Does Not Fit All</u>. AIGIS Publishers, 1993.

Orbach, Susie. <u>Fat is Feminist Issue I & 11. A Program to Conquer Compulsive Eating</u>. Berkley Book, l982.

Piper, Mary. <u>Hunger Pains</u>. Ballantine Books, 1997.

Radcliff, Rebecca Ruggles. <u>Enlightened Eating: Understand and Changing Your Relationship with Food</u>. Ease, 1996.

Rodin, Judith. <u>Body Traps</u>. William Morrow Co, Inc., 1993.

Roth, Geneen. <u>Breaking Free from Compulsive Eating</u>. Bobbs Merrill Co., l984.

Sandbek, Terence. <u>The Deadly Diet. Recovering from Anorexia and Bulimia</u>. New Harbinger Publication, 1996.

Stein, Patricia. <u>Anorexia Nervosa. Recovering Anorexics Tell Their Own Stories</u>. CompCare Publications, l986.

Virtue, Dorean. <u>Constant Craving: What Your Food Cravings Mean and How to Overcome Them</u>. Hay House, 1995.

Way, Karen. <u>Anorexia Nervosa and Recovery: Hunger for Meaning</u>. Harrington Park Press, 1993.

Winfrey, Oprah and Green, Bob. <u>Make the Connection. Ten Steps to a Better Body and a Better Life</u>. Hyperion,1996.

Whitalker & Davis. <u>The Bulimic College Student</u>. Haworth, 1989.

Zerbe, Katherine. <u>The Body Betrayed: Deeper Understanding of Women, Eating Disorders and Treatment</u>. Gürze Books, 1995.

PSYCHOLOGICAL SELF

Burns, David. Ten Days to Self-esteem. Macmillan, 1993.
Hall & Cohen. Self-Esteem. Tools for Recovery. Gürze Books, 1990.
Hall, Lindsey. Full Lives: Women Who Have Freed Themselves from Food and Weight Obsession. Gürze Books, 1993.
Jantz, Gregory. Hope, Help, Healing for Eating Disorders. Harold Shaw Publishers, 1995.
Johnson, Carol. Self-Esteem Comes in All Sizes: How to Be Happy & Healthy at Your Natural Weight. Doubleday, 1995.
Roth, Geneen. Appetites: on the Search for True Nourishment. Dutton Books, 1996.
Thayne and Markosian. Hope and Recovery. A Mother -Daughter Story about Anorexia Nervosa, Bulimia, and Manic Depression. Franklin Watts, 1992.
Tribole and Resch. Intuitive Eating: A Recovery Book for the Chronic Dieter. St. Martin Press, 1996.
Weiss, Laurie. An Action Plan for Your Inner Child: Parenting Each Other. Health Communications, 1991.

SEXUAL SELF

Davis, Laura. Courage to Heal Workbook: for Men and Women of Child Sexual Abuse. Harper and Row, 1990.
Meadow and Weiss. Good Girls Don't Eat Dessert: Changing Your Relationship to Food and Sex. Haworth Press, Inc., 1992.
Thompson, Becky. A Hunger So Wide and So Deep. American Women Speak Out on Eating Disorders. University of Minn. Press, 1994.
Schwartz, Mark & Leigh Cohn. Sexual Abuse and Eating Disorders. Brunner/Mazel Publishers, 1996.
Zerbe, Kathryn. The Body Betrayed: A Deeper Understanding of Women, Eating Disorders, and Treatment. Gürze Books, 1995.

SOCIAL SELF

Costin, Carolyn. Your Dieting Daughter. Brunner/Mazel Inc., 1997.
Costin, Carolyn. The Eating Disorder Sourcebook. Lowell House, 1997.
Goodman, Charisse W. The Invisible Women. Confronting Weight Prejudice in America. Gürze Books, 1995.

263

Hirschmann and Zaphiropoulous. <u>Preventing Childhood Eating Problems</u>. Gürze Books, 1993.

Krasnow, Micheal. <u>My Life as a Male Anorexic</u>. N.Y: Harrington Park Press, 1996.

Martin, Martin, Jeffers. <u>Is Your Family Making You Fat? How Your Family Affects Your Weight and What You Can Do About It</u>. Sulzburger and Graham Publishing Ltd., 1995.

Maine, Margo. <u>Father Hunger: Fathers, Daughters, and Food</u>. Gürze Books, 1991.

Piper, Mary. <u>Reviving Ophelia: Saving the Selves of Adolescent Girls</u>. Putman, 1994.

Roth, Geneen. <u>When Food is Love: Exploring the Relationship Between Eating and Intimacy</u>. Dutton, 1991.

Siegel, Brisman, & Weinshel. <u>Surviving an Eating Disorder. Strategies for Family and Friends</u>. N.Y. Harper & Row, 1989.

Waterhouse, Debra. <u>Like Mother, Like Daughter</u>. Hyperion Press, 1997.

SPIRITUAL SELF

Fodor, Viola. <u>Desperately Seeking Self: A Guidebook for People with Eating Disorders</u>, Gürze, 1997.

Latimer, Jane. <u>Beyond the Food Game. A Spiritual & Psychological Approach to Healing Emotional Eating</u>. Living Quest, 1993.

Rendida Ranch Staff. <u>Beyond the Looking Glass. Daily Devotions for Overcoming Anorexia and Bulimia</u>. Nashville: T. Nelson, 1992.

STRESSED SELF

Davis, Robbins, Eshelman, & McKay. <u>The Relaxation & Stress Reduction Workbook</u>. Oakland, CA: New Harbinger Publications, Inc., 1993.

Radcliffe, Rebecca Ruggles. <u>Dance Naked in Your Living Room: Handling Stress and Finding Joy</u>. Ease Co., 1997.

Wurtman, Judith. <u>Managing Your Mind and Mood Through Food: Enhance Performance, Handle Stress, Avoid Out of Control Eating</u>. Harper and Row, 1988.

Eating Disorders National Organizations

AABA   **American Anorexia/Bulimia Association**
293 Central Park W., #1R,
New York, NY 10024
(202) 510-8351

AED   **Academy for Eating Disorders**
Montefiore Medical School-Adolescent Medicine
111 East 210th St.
Bronx, NY 10467

ANAD   **Nat'l Ass. of Anorexia Nervosa & Associated Disorder**
P.O. Box 7
Highland Park, IL 60035
(847) 831-3438
http://members.aol.com/anad20/index.html

ANRED   **Anorexia Nervosa and Related Eating Disorder, Inc.**
P.O. Box 5102
Eugene, OR 97405
(514) 344-1144 or www.anred.com
http://www.anred.com

EDAP   **Eating Disorders Awareness and Prevention**
603 Stewart St., Suite 803
Seattle, WA 98101
(206) 382-3587
http://members.aol.com/cdapinc/home.html

IAEDP   **International Ass. of Eating Disorders Professionals**
123 NW 13th St. #206
Boca Raton, FL 33432-1618
(800) 800-8126

NEDO   **National Eating Disorders Organization**
6655 S. Yale Ave.
Tulsa, OK 74136
(918) 481-4044
http://www.laureate.com/nedo

Internet Information on Eating Disorders

Sites:

Alliance to Fight Eating Disorders- www.fsci.umu.edu/~AFED/
American Heart Association- http://www.amhrt.org/pubs/phoney.html
Anorexia Nervosa & Bulimia Association-//qlink.queensu.ca/~4map/
    anabhome.htm
Cathy's Eating Disorder Resources-www.stud.unit.no/studorg/ikstrh/ed
Eating Disorders Shared Awareness-http://www.mirror-mirror.org/eatdis.
    htm
Eating Disorder Programs- //members.aol.com/asedfaqqfaq5.html
Eating Disorders- www.vera.com/heritagehospital/eating.htm
Obesity & Weight Control- www.weight.com
Overeaters Recovery Home Page- www.hiwaay.net/recovery/
O.A.-http://www.scn.org/scripts/menus/o/oahow/menu/
Something Fishy's Eating Disorder- www.something-fishy.com/ed.htm
Weight Watchers.- Http://www.weight-watchers.com/
http://edrecovery.com/
http://www.dra.nl/~emmy/ased/index.html

Eating Disorder Newsgroups:

alt. food.fat-free: very low-fat
alt. food.low-fat:low-fat
alt.support.big-folks
alt.support.diet.rx
alt.support.eating-disord.
alt.support.obesity
alt.recovery.compulsive-eat
soc.support.fat-acceptance

Mailing Lists:
Eatdis (All kinds of eating disorders and their families/loved ones.)
CLUB-100 (For persons 100 lb. Or more overweight)
FATLOSS (Information and support for those wanting to lose body fat.)

I N D E X

About the Author

I have a passion for helping others with weight problems because of my own personal struggles. When I was in high school, I gained about fifty pounds and I didn't know what was happening to me. It was not until later that I became aware that my weight gain was related to an earlier sexual abuse incident. I thought no one would want to abuse me again if I put on weight.

During my early twenties, I not only lost the fifty pounds, but more. I became anorexic. I sometimes would eat a peach a day and exercise vigorously. I went from being overweight to being too thin. I never purged, only because, I never thought of it. Had I heard of purging, I would have tried it for I was desperate to be thin.

I once believed that my worth and my identity revolved solely around my weight. No matter what I weighed, I was never satisfied. Only when I was able to make the shifts that are mentioned in this book was I able to see and value my true worth.

As a professional counselor and university professor, I had always been successful in my career and wondered why I couldn't have this same success with my weight and looks. I was so critical of my weight and body that I was never satisfied with my appearance. When I learned to accept my body and weight, I learned not to be so critical of myself. When I looked internally at my worth, I became content and comfortable with being me. It was a relief to rid myself of the obsession with food and weight. It is my hope that this book will do the same for you.

I wish you well and would love your feedback. I hope to meet many of you on my book tours and at conferences I speak. If I can be more than what I weigh, you can too.

TO CONTACT THE AUTHOR

Sharon Sward
1231 S. Parker Rd. # 102
Denver, CO 80231
303-754-7095
SharoSward@aol.com

269